Can we pray for revival?

Can we pray for revival?
— towards a theology of revival

Brian H. Edwards

EVANGELICAL PRESS

EVANGELICAL PRESS
Faverdale North Industrial Estate, Darlington, DL3 0PH, England

Evangelical Press USA
P. O. Box 84, Auburn, MA 01501, USA

e-mail: sales@evangelical-press.org

web: http://www.evangelicalpress.org

First published 2001

British Library Cataloguing in Publication Data available

ISBN 0 85234 465 1

All Scripture quotations, unless otherwise indicated, are taken from the New King James Version. Copyright © 1982 by Thomas Nelson, Inc. Used by permission. All rights reserved.

Quotations marked 'NIV' are taken from the Holy Bible, New International Version. Copyright © 1973, 1978, 1984, International Bible Society. Used by permission of Hodder & Stoughton, a member of the Hodder Headline Group. All rights reserved.

Printed and bound in Great Britain by Creative Print & Design Wales, Ebbw Vale.

Revival is a sovereign work of God's Holy Spirit that produces an unusual awakening of spiritual life among God's people, resulting in an awesome awareness of God, a sincere repentance for sin, a deep longing for God and holiness, and an effective passion to reach the unsaved. It is generally accompanied by a significant number of the lost coming to true faith in Christ.

Contents

Introduction

In the spring of 1992 I was invited by the Faith Mission in Edinburgh to give the inaugural Duncan Campbell Lecture on the subject of revival. I set myself the discipline of using the four lectures to work out a theology of revival, and the principal at that time, Dr Colin Peckham, expressed a wish that the lectures be published. I suggested that I would like to spend more time working on the material and would hope to have it published in due course. Two or three times Colin enquired concerning my progress and, to my shame, I had to disappoint him on each occasion.

In the autumn of 1993 I repeated the material at the conference of the Fellowship for Revival in Swanwick, Derbyshire. But still I could find no time to review my work or expand it into a book. Two years later a change of ministry from my pastorate at Hook Evangelical Church saw me travelling throughout the United Kingdom, and this ruled out any possibility of returning to the task. The serious illness, and finally the home-call, of my wife Barbara meant that the whole project was set aside for some years. Only now, and with the encouragement of Evangelical Press, have I been able to reactivate it.

After writing *Revival! — a people saturated with God*[1], I was challenged with the comment, 'It's all right to look at so-called revival in history, but are you sure it is an experience to be sought and expected with the authority of Scripture behind it?' That is a fair question because there are many religious experiences among evangelical Christians, past and present, that bear little resemblance to anything taught or found in Scripture. If revival falls into that category, no matter how widespread, exciting, or apparently valuable it is, then we have no business with it. That is, unless we abandon our claim that the Bible is our infallible guide and our final test of all spiritual experience.

However, there is another equally important reason why we should be clear in our minds whether or not God has promised times of revival. Today, with varying degrees of urgency and understanding, Christians all over the world are pleading with God for an outpouring of his Holy Spirit in revival. The question is: on what do we base our plea? Has God given us the assurance that revival is a certainty because of his prophetic commitment to it? Or is it a probability providing we fulfil the right conditions? Or is it simply a possibility in the light of his character and the way that he has dealt with his people in the past? In other words, can we plead for revival with the support of the Bible? If so, on what ground can we plead? After all, God is not bound to honour promises he has not made.

In *Revival! — a people saturated with God* my purpose was to describe those experiences that have been labelled 'revival' and that have been enjoyed by parts of the Christian church, on and off, throughout its history. I tried to find the common ground between them. I looked for those things that connected them and for which they could be called revival. There were five that stood out above all others: an awesome sense of the presence of God, an overwhelming awareness of the seriousness of sin, an increasing longing for the knowledge of God, an unusual evidence of transformed lives, and a significant passion for the salvation of the lost. My book was therefore chiefly descriptive, and I searched the story of the church over a thousand years to see what God had been doing.

I did, however, base my search upon a Bible story that took place about seven hundred years before Christ. In doing this, I expressed my commitment to the view that revival is not an exclusively New Testament or post-Pentecost phenomenon. I hope that I demonstrated that all the significant ingredients of true revivals are found in the story of that remarkable visitation of God during the reign of Hezekiah, king of Judah. But if I am charged with the fact that I set my agenda from history and worked backward towards the Bible, then I have to plead partially guilty. Let me explain that qualified admission of guilt.

On the one hand, it is a fact that in the story of the church there have been times of special and unusual activity of the Holy Spirit that have been called revival, and I wanted to examine those periods of revival to see if they had any common ingredients that would help us to describe and define the word 'revival'. It was purely an historical search and as such it did not need to have any biblical roots. Hopefully it was useful as an end in itself. That there are periods of heightened spiritual activity and effectiveness throughout the history of the church is undeniable, whatever we make of them. But significant questions must follow. Are they biblical experiences? Can we expect them in our own day? Should we pray for them? How would we recognize them in biblical terms? Does the Bible give us hope for regular revivals and/or for a great end-of-time revival? These are all questions that demand answers, and they can only properly be answered from Scripture itself. It is answering these questions that is the purpose of this book. In setting down my position at last, I express my appreciation to the staff at the Faith Mission, Edinburgh, for their invitation to me towards the end of the last century and for their long patience with me since then!

This book is therefore a contribution to the ongoing discussion of the biblical basis for revival. I am confident that others will criticize it, correct it and improve upon it. But it is essential that on this issue, as on all issues concerning the health of the Christian church, our confidence and expectation should not rest upon history or experience but upon the clear teaching and

example of God's Word. The more I have read Scripture with
this subject in mind, the more I have become confident that
revival is a biblical experience that God has given to his people
frequently throughout the history of Israel and the early church.
But more than this, I believe he has told us something about
the nature of revival that is vital for today's Christians to
understand.

However, whenever we approach this subject we should do
so with a sense of awe and wonder. The work of God in revival, as is true of every work of his, is always greater than our
finite minds can grasp; we must be on our guard that we do not
box God in more than the limits that he has set for himself in
his Word. In other words, we can produce a systematic theology for revival that by its narrowness refuses to allow anything to be revival that does not perfectly fit *our* system. On the
other hand, this does not mean that anything goes. Whilst God
will never allow *us* to dictate the parameters of revival, he has
certainly set his own; and some of these are clearly revealed in
his Word. Iain Murray in his excellent book *Pentecost — Today?*
makes this point well, 'Those who have seen great revivals have
been the first to say there was so much that left them amazed
and conscious of mystery.'[2] This book, together with his *Revival
and Revivalism*, (Banner of Truth, 1994), are two valuable contri-
butions to the subject of revival and should be read by all with
a concern for the subject. As will be seen, I take a different view
from Murray on the use of the Old Testament, but I nevertheless warmly commend his work.

Unfortunately the word 'revival' is used so loosely today
that there seems to be little point in continuing with our study
until at least we understand a definition. I may be criticized for
dealing with definitions before I have arrived at my biblical
models, but much of the Christian world has become so confused that at least it will be helpful to set out what I do not mean
when I use the word 'revival'.

1. Revival is not to be confused with mission

Too often the word 'revival' refers either to a series of evangelistic meetings, or to a mission for the deepening of the spiritual
life of the church members. This is often how it is used in North
America. In this sense it is something that is organized by the
church and, like a wise military commander, the church can
choose the ground on which it fights. A revival is planned; it is
staged. We start it, and we stop it when we want it to stop.
James Orr, the historian of revival, used to illustrate this by the
example of two churches in the same town in America each
boasting a poster that advertised revival meetings. One claimed,
'Revival here every Monday night', whilst the other assured
passers-by, 'Revival here every night except Monday'. That
clearly reveals the idea that revival is something we manufacture.
We stage it and manage it with careful precision.

During the 1830s, the American evangelist, Charles
Grandison Finney, modelled what has become widely accepted
as the definition of revival in North America. Whilst he undoubtedly saw many thousands converted to Christ through
his preaching, Finney gradually turned the means that he
employed in his meetings into a methodology for all to copy;
this was particularly true of the 'altar call' which pressed for an
immediate and open response to the preaching. Finney gave a
series of lectures in 1834 and they were published the following
year. Their danger lies in the fact that they are often accurate,
persuasively attractive — and yet fundamentally flawed.

Finney's analysis of the state of much of the professing church
was at times very incisive, and he rightly emphasized the need
for costly self-examination[3], the vital place of prayer[4] and the
quality of the lives of Christians to support the preaching of the
Word. All these are necessary ingredients if we are serious about
true revival. Even his description of the hallmarks of revival is
almost unimprovable. It includes: a conviction of sin among

Christians and their repentance and renewal of faith, their love for others issuing in an evangelistic zeal, an appreciation of the reality of heaven accompanied by a loosening grip upon the world, and finally the salvation of many sinners.

However, the danger of his legacy is that Finney was fundamentally in error. His *Lectures on Theology*[5] reveal how far he differed from the 'reformed theology' of, for example, Jonathan Edwards whom he vigorously attacked. Finney's theology was thoroughly man-centred. He believed that we are not born into a state of sin (he denied 'original sin'), and that men and women therefore have 'a natural ability to obey God'.[6] He denied what Luther called 'the bondage of the will'; he denied the sovereign initiative of God in election; and he denied the full security of believers (the final perseverance of the saints). For him justification was neither forensic nor judicial, nor (necessarily) eternal, and the righteousness of Christ was not imputed to the sinner. All these doctrines he declared to be 'better fitting a romance than a system of theology'.[7] In fact, Finney used orthodox language to describe theology but invested much of it with a wholly new meaning — a meaning often peculiar to himself.

Significantly for our subject, in his lectures on revival Finney denied that conversion was the result of regeneration; rather it was the result of moral persuasion. This meant that he confused the author of any true spiritual work with the agent that God might use. Finney claimed that 'As an agent God works in two ways'. Those two ways were his providential interference in circumstances and the direct influence of his Holy Spirit. That may appear orthodox until we realize that Finney thought of God as merely one agent among at least two others. The messenger is equally an agent as is the sinner himself. It is the entirely free interplay of each of these that may, or may not, achieve the salvation of the sinner. On the one hand, Finney states clearly that Christians 'must realize their complete dependence upon the Holy Spirit or their efforts will fail' but immediately adds, 'If Christians start to believe that God is necessary because sinners are *unable* to obey, or that God is obligated to give his Holy Spirit in order to make sinners *able* to obey the gospel, they insult God and their prayers will fail' (italics original).[8] This prepared the ground for his insistence that revivals can be induced by the employment of the correct techniques (he called them 'the constituted means').

In 1832, two years before Finney first gave his lectures on this subject, William Sprague, a Presbyterian minister and graduate of Yale and Princeton, had published his own *Lectures on Revivals of Religion*. In it he used this same division of providence and the Spirit. Typically, Finney was deliberately responding from his own perspective. Whilst Finney covered some of the same territory as Sprague, the two men came from a very different theological perspective. For example, whilst both men spoke of human responsibility, Sprague wrote of the 'agency of the Spirit in performing the change' in the sinner's heart.[9] That was an admission Finney would not make. For him, the Spirit could influence, but not accomplish the change. Sprague also warned against 'substituting human inventions for divinely appointed means' and concluded, 'Brethren, we honour the Holy Spirit most, when we give him precisely the place which he claims; when we recognize him as the efficient author of conviction, conversion and sanctification; but he is offended when we undertake to palm upon him what we ought to take with shame to ourselves.'[10] Sprague also argued that the end does not justifies the means, and that physical responses are not necessarily evidence of a spiritual conversion. Unquestionably the Princeton graduate was warning against the so-called 'new measures' that Finney had been promoting for some years.

Finney entirely misrepresented, or to be charitable perhaps he simply misunderstood, the theology of those he criticized. He maintained that the Reformed view of the sovereignty of God (represented by Sprague and Edwards before him) meant

that we can only trust God and do nothing; and that the church
has no more influence in producing a revival 'than in producing
thunder, hail or an earthquake'. Sprague had actually used similar language himself,[11] but he knew that a true understanding of
God's sovereignty has never taken a passive view. By confusing
the author (God) with the agent (man), Finney was free virtually to dispense with the author and focus upon the activity of
the agent. He condemned the idea that 'Promoting religion is
somehow so mysterious a subject of divine sovereignty, that
there is no connection between the means and the end.' In
fact, the Reformed theology that he so despised had never
doubted that God is both God of the end and the means to the
end. Finney's theology of means and ends is stated simply,
'There is one fact under the government of God of universal
notice and of everlasting remembrance which is, that the most
useful and important things are most easily and certainly
obtained by the use of the appropriate means.'[12] In other words,
if the church does the right things, blessing (revival) will inevitably follow.

   Whilst there is truth and value in many parts of his twenty-
two lectures on revival, it was this man-centred approach that
slowly formed the understanding of the word revival over much
of the world. Finney was convinced that if the church met the
correct requirements then the desired result would inevitably
follow: 'The law connecting cause and effect is more undeviating
in spiritual than in natural things, and so there are fewer ex-
ceptions.'[13] He concluded that the only way for the church to
advance is by periodic 'excitements' and that revival was not a
miracle in the sense of 'Divine interference' but 'a purely philo-
sophical result of the right use of the constituted means.'[14]

   If the study of revival in North America had dealt justly with
another preacher, who was arguably of even greater value than
Finney, the present understanding might be better. Asahel
Nettleton was almost ten years Finney's senior and he saw tens

of thousands converted under his preaching. However, whilst Nettleton was a household name in America early in the nineteenth century, today he appears to be unknown to many books and exhibitions on the history of evangelism and revival on that continent. Nettleton held a high view of the sovereignty of God and strongly opposed Finney's theology and methods. He was a man of passionate prayer and earnest preaching; yet he was convinced that both revival and regeneration were sovereign works of God, and that man should never dare to try to manipulate the work of the Spirit. He took issue with Finney but, weakened by typhus fever, he predeceased Finney by three decades; and though he established a seminary to train preachers, he left no lectures, no books, and few printed sermons. One of his biographers laments, 'By the turn of the twentieth century his name and life had fallen into oblivion.'[15] It was therefore left to Finney to dominate the American mindset on the subject of revival to the present day. In the course of time, revival, which Finney understood as the inevitable outcome of correct human endeavour, became synonymous with the enthusiastic endeavour itself.[16]

In the sovereignty of God, Finney's methods did not hinder God from working in true revival across America and subsequently across large tracts of the world following the Fulton Street prayer meetings of 1857.[17] Nor did it hinder a real work of God among both Union and Confederate armies during the American Civil War. But it did leave the legacy that many have come to believe that revivals can be 'worked up'. A widespread reading of the life of Nettleton, the lectures of Sprague and the works of Jonathan Edwards would re-establish a correct view of revival. Richard F. Lovelace in *Dynamics of Spiritual Life*, writes, 'It is not too strong a statement to contend that the whole career of evangelicalism in America would have been cleansed of its distinctive scandals if Edwards had remained alive in the memory of the revivalists'.[18]

2. Revival is not to be confused with either phenomena or excitement

Since writing my first book on the subject of revival — though I am not suggesting because of it — there has been an increased longing for revival across many parts of the Christian church. I have heard of a number of prayer meetings that have been established to pray for this very thing. This bodes hopefully for the future.

There are a variety of reasons behind this renewed interest in revival. Some are driven by their postmillennial theology that anticipates a golden age prior to the return of Christ. They expect that gospel success will soon cover the world 'as the waters cover the sea'. Consequently, among some, the 'prophets' have prophesied specific revivals in specific places and at specific times; leaders have manipulated large and small events to replicate what they think revival would be like. Strange and noisy phenomena have stirred confusion into the quiet waters of longing and expectation. These things were advertised as 'rumours of revival' and people were assured that great things were on the way. In reality these weird phenomena were not the outskirts of revival at all and great things were not on the way. Nothing of lasting significance has happened to the lost community around those growling, giggling congregations. The phenomena came and went and reappeared in a new guise, like all man-made attempts to ape the work of God. The stir that they cause has been in the church, but not in the world. The devil and the world joined in the laughter, but from a very different perspective!

I have been encouraged by five reprints of *Revival!*, and for the responses that have come to me from all over the world. There have been few criticisms and only one that I would like to mention in order to set the record straight. In a gracious letter, Dr Herbert McGonigle from the Nazarene Theological College in Manchester, England, challenged my statement that in the revival early in the eighteenth century John Wesley prayed for phenomena. Dr McGonigle is right. Whilst all would agree that at first Wesley did not actively discourage some of the phenomena that occurred in his meetings, there would appear to be no positive evidence that he actually prayed for such things. This correction only serves to underline the fact that few leaders in true revival focused upon the phenomena. Sadly, it is our existentially-driven society that is more interested in the ridiculous than the relevant. To compare the relatively minor intrusions of bizarre behaviour in the time of Wesley to the widespread encouragement of such things today betrays an ignorance of both Scripture and history.

Jonathan and Sarah Edwards have been dragged from their obscurity, as far as many Christians are concerned, and have been superficially read and used to support experiences that Edwards himself, one of the greatest minds and wisest pastors America has ever produced, would never have endorsed. I am aware that in revival strange things may happen, and we have already said that we cannot box God in. To cavil at the work of God simply because we do not approve of all his ways is a sure way to miss what God has for us. Here is one example of this danger. In 1865 William Hamilton published *An Inquiry into the Scriptural Character of the Revival of 1859* in Ulster.[19] He critically analysed the physical responses observed in the Ulster awakening and concluded that the Spirit was not at work in this so-called revival. But his copious references to Scripture tied God to an inflexible regime. Revival is full of the unexpected, and leaders need unusual wisdom to discern the true from the counterfeit. Hamilton was convinced that the Spirit 'never did and never will produce such distress' as was experienced by many under conviction of sin in the 1859 revival in Ulster. But that takes little notice of Psalm 38!

Spurgeon may have referred to revival as a time of 'glorious disorder', and others think of it as 'a great confusion', but when the focus is upon the disorder and the confusion and these are cited as proof of the genuineness of the experience, then we can be sure someone has lost his way. It is as wrong therefore to dismiss a work of God because of the presence of certain unbiblical phenomena as it is to use such phenomena as evidence that it is a work of God.

Unfortunately the desperate desire among some today for evidence of God being at work, has led to a devaluing of the word 'revival' in the United Kingdom also. The awesome otherness of revival has, for many, been replaced by the ordinary. We are learning to introduce our own constituted means to obtain results that may give a veneer of spiritual life. To advertise a 'revival' meeting at Wembley in London in 1995 a full colour brochure was widely distributed. The meeting promised to be 'a significant time in this growing revival'. More to the point, a significant attraction was undoubtedly to be found in the 'cinema-style large-screen projections, intelligent lighting, 10k surround sound and total UV coverage'. All this was described as 'the wind of revival and the Spirit's revival dynamics'. Participants were encouraged to 'Dare to say, "It's Revival"' and to believe that 'From all over the UK there is news! Of Christian revival! Not just "refreshing" — "revival!" ' It is not difficult to appreciate how the many thousands who are caught up in meetings like this will cultivate an altogether different idea of the word 'revival' from that which is presented to us in Scripture, and even in the history of the church. Those who attend such meetings are encouraged to believe that they have been to a revival meeting. But even a prayer meeting for revival that is devoid of hype but filled with the presence of the Spirit must not be assumed to be revival itself.

Another lasting effect of much of the current scene is that many have built up an indifference to failed prophecy. Revivals that were due to begin in specific places and at specific times have failed to materialize, but thousands shrug off the failed prophecies and, short on memory and long on tolerance, they remain loyal to those who chatter from their own imagination. The only alternative is to convince ourselves that we have seen the outskirts of revival when clearly we have not. Modern-day 'prophets' are rarely successful — but who cares? As Peter Jensen remarked some years ago when describing modern-day prophecy, 'If it is true it is not significant, and if it is significant it is not true.'

3. Revival is not to be confused with restoration

For some, revival is the restoration of certain spiritual gifts to the life of the church. This is the position of the Charismatic Renewal movement and, although it has undergone some modification in recent years, originally charismatic renewal was seen as the revival of all revivals. The restoration of what have become known as 'charismatic gifts' to the life of the churches are seen as the great outcrop of true spiritual revival. Through publications and articles, some of those within the Restoration movement made it clear that when the great revival comes it will be charismatic, baptistic and non-denominational. An interesting thought when we consider that the last revival that took place in the United Kingdom was non-charismatic, paedo-baptist and within the Church of Scotland! I am referring to the times of revival under the ministry of Duncan Campbell during the 1940s and 1950s in the Western Islands of Scotland. Before that, the last revival in England was in East Anglia in 1921; this was non-charismatic and denominational, but at least it began in a Baptist church!

We are all tempted to suggest to God the kind of revival that would most suit our personal preference or theology. I have done it myself. If given the choice, St Peter's, Dundee, 1839 would suit me excellently! But if there is one thing we learn about revival it is that God is in control, and he does according

to his will. In fact, revival usually begins to wane when men try
to take over from God. In *Revival!*, I wrote briefly of the 'Error,
excess and the unusual in revival'. A whole book could be written on this subject alone. But it is a simple fact of history, both
within the Bible and outside it, that the so-called 'charismatic
gifts', whatever their value may or may not be, have rarely
been evident in spiritual revival — it is therefore unwise to insist
upon them at this late stage in the story of the church. The
influential Azusa Street revival of 1906 in Los Angeles is often
cited as an exception to this claim. However, the leaders of the
Apostolic Faith Mission were Pentecostal in theology prior to
the revival, and where charismatic gifts are expected they will
often be found in revival. The article on Azusa Street in the
Dictionary of Pentecostal and Charismatic Movements (ed.
Burgess and McGee, Regency, Zondervan, 1988) claims that
speaking in tongues was 'high on the agenda' from the earliest
days of the revival and that 'Restorationism' was one of its
formative influences.[20] The converse is equally true, which
demonstrates that they are no part of the essential definition or
description of revival. A point that I made in *Revival!*.[21]

4. Revival is not to be confused with reformation

Reformation is a re-forming of the doctrine or structure of the
church to the theology of the New Testament. I do not deny
that reformation has often been accompanied by revival; this
was certainly the case during the time of the Reformation across
Europe in the fifteenth and sixteenth centuries. Nor do I deny
that revival often leads to reformation; this happened to a degree
following the eighteenth-century revival in England. But whereas
reformation is primarily to do with doctrine — what we believe,
revival is primarily to do with life — how we behave. Perhaps

one of the clearest examples of this in the Bible is found in the difference between what happened during the reigns of Hezekiah and Josiah. Hezekiah, who was without doubt a leader, experienced revival because it was essentially a movement among the people. Under Josiah, on the other hand, changes were imposed from the top. A similar contrast may be found in the time of Ezra where the response of the people was unanimous and wholehearted, whereas under Nehemiah the people's reaction appears to have been largely due to the governor's firm and godly leadership, though later I will suggest that there was revival in the time of Nehemiah.

Of course revival will affect doctrine. If a man doubts the authority of Scripture or the reality of eternal hell prior to revival, he will soon have his mind changed when the Spirit comes. But people with a loose theology — I do not mean heretical theology, there is a difference between error and heresy — can be revived and remain loose in their theology. How else are we to explain the difference between, for example, Charles Grandison Finney on the one hand and Asahel Nettleton on the other? Both of them were preaching in times of revival in the early nineteenth century in America, but each held a significantly different theology from the other. How do we explain the difference between John Wesley and George Whitefield? Both were preaching during a time of revival in the eighteenth century and both were greatly used by God, but each held a fundamentally different theology when it came to the doctrine of the sovereignty of God in election, sanctification and eternal security.

If it is suggested that the line between true revival and true reformation is too close to call, then I would not argue. I believe that there can be the one without the other, but ideally the two are handmaids of each other. My only point here is that they are two different things.

5. Revival is not to be confused with renewal

The evangelical world is full of experiences today. They are
certainly not all bad, but even the experience that leads the
Christian to a deeper awareness of the reality of Christ is not in
itself revival. A renewal of spiritual life for a believer or for a
church ought not to be unfamiliar in the experience of Christians; but this is not revival. Nor is it necessarily revival when
men and women are being converted in a way not normally
experienced. There was a time when the word 'renewal' would
adequately describe what is meant by revival; however, the word
has been used today to cover so many experiences that it is no
longer serviceable as a synonym for revival. Richard Lovelace
in *Dynamics of Spiritual Life*, (IVP USA, 1979), uses the word
renewal to refer to revival, and J. I. Packer follows him in *God
in our Midst — Seeking and Receiving Ongoing Revival*, (Word
Publishing, 1987).

Erroll Hulse helpfully reminds us that an older word to describe this kind of thing is a 'visitation'.[22] He pleads for a careful
use of terminology, but is perhaps too restrictive in suggesting
that 'Strictly speaking, it is better to describe a local revival as a
visitation.' How local is 'local'? It is arbitrary to define revivals
by geography. Revival is what God does, not where he does it.

Preaching under the heading of 'What is Revival?', C. H.
Spurgeon wisely reminded his nineteenth-century congregation
that not every Christian should always be crying for revival:

> Feeding and lying down in green pastures and led by the
> still waters, they ought not always to be crying, 'My lean-
> ness, my leanness, woe unto me!' Sustained by gracious
> promises and enriched out of the fullness which God has
> treasured up in his dear Son, their souls should prosper
> and be in health, and their piety ought to need no reviving.

They should aspire to a higher blessing, a richer mercy,
than a mere revival. They should be asking for growth in
grace, for increase of strength, and for greater success.

For a man who believed passionately in revival, 'a mere
revival' is a strange expression! Can there be anything more
successful than revival? However, perhaps Spurgeon touches a
vital note here. A longing for revival should not primarily be for
the benefit of God's people but for the honour of God himself.
A cry for revival is not because we are dry, but because by
being dry God and his Son Jesus Christ are not honoured. The
highest motive for a longing for revival is expressed in Isaiah
26:8, 'The desire of our soul is for your name and for the remembrance of you.' Anything else is unworthy. God may satisfy our
thirst and renew our zeal without necessarily giving revival. We
must learn to be a people satisfied with God even when we are
not yet saturated with God. A satisfied dissatisfaction is one of
those necessary paradoxes of the Christian life.

Besides, revival should never be the all-consuming concern
of the church. Good things can happen for the church and
through the church, even on the outside of revival. Both personally and corporately there is such a thing as a church renewed
without revival. The prayer meeting that insists on revival or
nothing at all, is in grave danger of receiving and achieving the
latter. The nineteenth-century Methodists believed that without
periodic revival the church would die. I admire their passion
but doubt their wisdom. Finney went further by claiming, 'Nothing but a revival of religion can prevent the means of grace
from doing great injury to the ungodly. Without a revival they
will grow harder and harder under preaching, and will experience a more horrible damnation than they would if they had
never heard the gospel. Your children and your friends will go
down to a much more horrible fate in hell, in consequence of

the means of grace, if there are no revivals to convert them to God. Better were it for them if there were no means of grace, no sanctuary, no Bible, no preaching, than to live and die where there is no revival.'[23] Again, I cannot help agreeing with Finney's concern and motive but he has, as he did so often, overstated his case. The opposite of revival is not inevitable spiritual hardness and death.

It is this kind of thinking that has compelled many American churches to organize 'revival' meetings because of the fear that the alternative is the demise of their church. The same thing is beginning to happen in the United Kingdom too. Finney believed that 'nothing but revival can preserve a church from annihilation'. That may be good rhetoric, but with all my heartlonging and theological commitment to revival I believe it is neither accurate nor helpful. There *is* renewal apart from revival. Perhaps this distinction is more important than we recognize. If God will not yet bring revival then he surely must want his people to be constantly renewed in heart, mind and spirit according to his Word.

6. Revival is not to be confused with church growth

The church growth movement has become big business today, and leaders are constantly encouraged to attend one conference or another in order to learn how their church can grow. And grow we must, because there is no place in our success-orientated society for the Christian community that does not make numerical progress. Successful means big, and big means influential.

This is not the place for a critique of the church growth movement, but the reasons why a church grows are far too numerous to be limited to neat formulae. The contemporary style of worship, the personality of the leader, 'attractive' theology (or lack of it), well-run programmes, a careful application of the results of social demographics, and smart marketing, are just a few of the ingredients that may cause a church to grow. Some have confused this with revival. The fact that a congregation increases from fifteen to five hundred in five years — or even five months — is not in itself evidence of revival. Whilst it is true that revival always results in numerical growth, there are far more important factors that indicate whether or not the work can be described as revival. Some of the most significant of these were introduced in *Revival!*, and they will be rediscovered as we look at revival in the Bible.

Sadly, some of our contemporary church growth 'successes' have masked the real need for spiritual revival. Our numbers, programmes, budgets and buildings are all evidence that we are doing well and that little more is required. In the bookshop of one of the largest evangelical churches in America that is a model for church growth, I looked in vain for books on the subject of revival. But then, why should they need such a thing? Some leaders of mega-churches admit that they have little or no theology of revival. This is, of course, understandable. When we are gaining ground and doing well there appears to be little need for anything more than more of the same that caused us to get where we are. What this reveals is how superficial our assessment of the health of a local church often is. In the wisdom of God we have no idea of the numerical size of the churches in Revelation 2 - 3, but we are left in no doubt about the spiritual condition of each of them. There is a vital lesson for us to learn there.

What is revival?

I have come to the conclusion that no single definition of revival will do. To describe a particular revival is easy, but to define revival as a noun is almost impossible. In a wise caution against over-exact definitions, Iain Murray suggests that 'If we could understand revivals, they would not be the astonishing things which they are.'[24] Similarly, J. I. Packer warns that because of the different cultures in which the church finds itself in different ages, and the various ways in which it has lost its vitality, 'It is not safe for us to assume that the outward forms and phenomena of revival in this or any future age will always prove to have exact historical precedents.'[25] In other words, as we said earlier in this introduction, revivals do not all conform to a set pattern. However, far from this being a discouraging start, it is in fact the glory of revival. It is an act of God's sheer sovereignty, and because he has nowhere in the Bible provided us with a simple definition of the experience, his Spirit is as free as the wind to blow wherever, whenever and however he pleases.

This insistence that God is free to work in his own way in revival, does not mean to imply that at such a time anything goes — far from it. The relationship between the Spirit and the Word must never be divorced. The Holy Spirit will never work in a way that is condemned by, or contrary to, his own revelation in Scripture. One reason why the church in ordinary times needs to attend to sound doctrine (Titus 2:1) is so that the human excesses and errors that so frequently slip into times of revival will be identified and rejected — early and firmly.

In my earlier book I made the point that the word 'revival' is easier to describe than to define. When definitions are attempted, they generally refer to the preceding time of spiritual coldness, ineffectiveness or lethargy among the people of God — the church. Generally that is a fair assumption and certainly most of the biblical revivals reveal that. On the other hand, it is not always true that the first work of the Spirit is to 'revive' a dying church. If Pentecost is seen as the revival to which the Old Testament prophets looked forward in longing, we must not forget that on this occasion the Spirit worked first for the conversion of thousands of unsaved Jews and proselytes.

Therefore whilst the word 'revival' implies a 're-viving' of a life that is dying, we must not allow our word to preclude those occasions when God's chief purpose is to resurrect the dead. Unusual and untypical that may be, but then, revival is the unusual.

In the light of the above caveats and cautions, I would *describe* revival as a sovereign work of God's Holy Spirit that produces an unusual awakening of spiritual life among God's people, resulting in an awesome awareness of God, a sincere repentance for sin, a deep longing for God and holiness, and an effective passion to reach the unsaved. It is generally accompanied by a significant number of the lost coming to true faith in Christ. But I still cannot *define* revival better than in the words of Duncan Campbell, 'a people saturated with God'. Some have objected to that phrase, but I cannot think of a more accurate way of defining my understanding of revival. Revival is big, radical, unusual, always God initiated and always God honouring.

Because this is intended as a biblical and theological contribution to such an important subject, I have denied both the reader and myself the enjoyment of including references to historic revivals. This is not because such allusions are unimportant — far from it. We can hardly tell the next generation things 'our fathers have told us' so that 'they should make them known to their children' (Psalm 78:3-6), unless we first read what our fathers have told us! On the other hand, if we cannot discuss this subject of revival from the Bible alone, without falling back on the anecdotes of history, then perhaps we are making too much of it. The Bible is our final authority and controlling guide. If there are hallmarks of revival, we must find them in Scripture and not first from history; and if there are warnings against error, these too must be drawn from the Bible and not from our cultural preferences.

The purpose of this book is to answer the questions: 'Is such an experience to be found in Scripture?' and, 'Do the Scriptures expect revival for the future?' We generally assume that we know the answer to these questions, but before the end of this book there may be some surprises. Initially we will confine ourselves to the Old Testament. In the next chapter I want to show that to speak of revival as an Old Testament experience does not challenge the uniqueness of Pentecost. In the chapters following I will deal with revival in the Old Testament in three ways: the examples of the Old Testament, the experience of the Old Testament and the expectation of the Old Testament. In other words, can we find revival in the Old Testament? If so, what do we learn from it? And is revival part of the longing and expectation of the Old Testament prophets?

1.

The Holy Spirit in the Old Testament

In this chapter I want to examine the work of the Holy Spirit in the Old Testament and compare it with his work after Pentecost. My conclusion in part will be that all the chief aspects of his work are present under the old covenant. The importance of this is that if we establish that the Spirit was significantly at work under the old covenant, it will be a short step to agree that, even at that time, revival was one of God's ways of working among his people. I am aware that not everyone will accept my conclusion because it appears to involve a narrowing of the gap in the work of the Spirit between the two covenants. In declaring my belief that it is correct to speak of revival during the Old Testament era, it is unavoidable that we enter one of the more difficult, though least debated areas of the work of the Spirit, namely, what is the difference between his work before and after Pentecost?

A well-used text for revival is found in 2 Chronicles 7:14: 'If my people who are called by my name will humble themselves, and pray and seek my face, and turn from their wicked ways, then I will hear from heaven, and will forgive their sin and heal their land.' However, a case has been made that this verse cannot properly be used in prayer for revival. This is an issue of considerable significance because if such a verse falls, many others will fall with it. There are at least three arguments against its use.

The first argument against the use of 2 Chronicles 7:14 in connection with revival is that this promise, and others like it, is limited to the old covenant promises associated with the land of Israel. Writing on this subject, John Armstrong claims, 'These simply cannot be promises of new effusions of the Spirit upon the church.'[1] Armstrong provides an excellent analysis of the subject of revival with which I am in large agreement. However, on this issue I would go further than him. Strictly speaking, I agree with this statement. We cannot take it as a specific promise of revival in the church at any particular time. However, there are two important principles that we must not overlook. Firstly, when God spoke to Israel — and in particular to Judah and Jerusalem — he was speaking to his chosen people; the new covenant equivalent of Israel is the church. Therefore, this verse *can* be taken as a prayer for God to restore the church to its proper glory. Secondly, whilst not everything God says to Israel can be applied to the church today — there were sometimes specific promises of events to come — nevertheless by observing his dealings with his chosen people, we can always learn something of the character of God.

I suggest that what we learn from this passage in Chronicles is that God will return to his people in forgiveness and spiritual healing when they sincerely turn to him. In other words, whilst it is certainly true that we cannot take this passage as a specific promise of specific revival at any given time, it is a promise of God's unchanging care for his people, and a statement about the way in which he cares. The principle enshrined here is that God will respond to a genuinely humble and repentant people. No nation today stands in the same covenant relationship to God as Israel did in the Old Testament. However, Christians in any nation can plead with God to heal their land from its spiritual and moral decline on the ground of Jeremiah 29:7: 'And seek the peace of the city where I have caused you to be carried away captive, and pray to the LORD for it; for in its peace you will have peace.' On the other hand, we must never presume that we have a *covenant* claim upon God for this.

As an analogy we may refer to the many promises of forgiveness that are found in the Old Testament. Micah 7:18-19 is a good example:

> Who is a God like you,
> pardoning iniquity
> and passing over the transgression of
> the remnant of his heritage?
> He does not retain his anger for ever,
> because he delights in mercy.
> He will again have compassion on us,
> and will subdue our iniquities.
> You will cast all our sins
> into the depths of the sea.

In its immediate context Micah appeals for God's forgiving grace to the faithful in Israel — 'the remnant of his heritage'. God had a covenant commitment to this remnant. But God still has a covenant commitment to his people — the church which is the new 'remnant'. However, when Christians take this as a principle of God's willingness to forgive all who come in true repentance, their plea is not on the ground of God's covenant promises to faithful Israel of old, but on the ground that this is a revelation of the character of God as a forgiving God. In the same way, God's promises of reviving his people Israel are a revelation of his character as a reviving God.

A second argument against the use of Old Testament promises to Israel is that we cannot properly use the word 'revival' to refer to anything that happened in the Old Testament, because in God's unfolding revelation throughout the Old Testament there is a deeper understanding and experience that is reserved for Pentecost. Revival is seen therefore as a uniquely New

Testament experience, and it is suggested that we flatten this uniqueness by using the word for any experience recorded in the Old Testament. Iain Murray in *Pentecost Today?* quotes the warning of Sinclair Ferguson against 'flattening the contours of redemptive history.'[2] But Ferguson himself appears not to forbid the use of the word revival to refer to events in the Old Testament. On the contrary, he quotes Jonathan Edwards approvingly when Edwards says that 'It may be observed that from the Fall of man to our day, the work of redemption in its effects has mainly been carried on by remarkable communications of the Spirit of God. Though there be a more constant influence of God's Spirit always in some degree attending his ordinances, yet the way in which the greatest things have been done towards carrying on the work always has been by remarkable effusions at special seasons of mercy.' Ferguson wisely observes that 'Any biblical theology of the Spirit's work must recognize the progressive and cumulative character of historical revelation.'[3] I do not wish to overlook that warning.

The problem with Murray's position is that if the word 'revival' is not allowed as a description of an Old Testament experience, we must ask whether we should place the same limitation on such words as 'regeneration', 'conversion' or 'salvation'. Presumably some would. Charles Ryrie claims that 'The permanent indwelling of the Spirit is distinctive to this age and was not experienced in the Old Testament.'[4] If this is so, we need to explain how men and women in the Old Testament could have true saving faith without a new birth that involved a permanently indwelling Holy Spirit.

I want to show in this chapter that, among much else, we can rightly speak of spiritual gifts before Pentecost even though these concepts did not reach their full revelation until the new covenant. Also, we may ask, was the writer to the Hebrews flattening contours when he commented that Moses counted 'esteeming the reproach of Christ greater riches than the treasures of Egypt'? After all, it is doubtful whether Moses understood the fuller significance of those treasures.

A third argument against the use of Old Testament promises of revival is that whilst the verb 'revive' is used in the Old Testament, the noun never appears; therefore, it is claimed, we cannot correctly use the word 'revival' before Pentecost. This argument is a *non sequitur* or logical fallacy, if only because there are other nouns that do not appear in the Old Testament. The noun 'justification' is one example. Yet the apostle Paul had no scruple in using that word to refer to an Old Testament experience. When Abraham 'believed in the LORD and [God] accounted it to him for righteousness' (Genesis 15:6), he was, according to Paul, justified by faith in the sense understood in the New Testament. In Romans 4:3 and also verse 22 Paul makes a neat jump from the verb 'accounted' to the noun 'justification' and adds that these Old Testament events were written for us also because Christ died and rose 'for our justification' (NIV). The noun 'justification' nowhere appears in the Old Testament in the context of our relationship with God, and yet it is clear that Paul sees that what we receive by faith is precisely what Abraham received by faith — namely, justification. Similarly, the nouns 'reform' and 'reformation' do not appear in the Old Testament, but how else can we describe what happened in the time of Josiah or Nehemiah? As is well recognized, the New Testament itself lacks nouns for 'Trinity' and 'Incarnation', but we do not deny that the concepts are there.

From the perspective of the position that I take, this debate is crucial. If we cannot use the word 'revival' to refer to an Old Testament experience then it effectively places an embargo on the use of any Old Testament narrative or promise which could help us in our search for a theology of revival. It also effectively dispenses with my biblical substructure in *Revival! — a people saturated with God*, where I used the spiritual awakening of Judah in the time of King Hezekiah to illustrate aspects of revival found in the history of the Christian church. On the other hand, I do agree that we must maintain a distinction between the work of the Spirit before and after Pentecost. There are both similarities and differences; what is called continuity and dis-continuity. This is the subject that will be the focus of this chapter.

It is common to argue that the difference between the normal life of the church and the state of revival is one of degree and measure — not a difference in kind.[5] I am not altogether happy with this distinction. In this chapter I will set out what I believe to be the fundamental similarities and differences in the work of the Holy Spirit under the old and new covenants. But I will anticipate one conclusion here. I believe that when we are think-ing of the contrasting work of the Spirit between the old and new covenants, we are wiser not to speak of either degree or kind, but of dynamic and purpose, or perhaps better still, potential.

The Holy Spirit in the Old Testament — continuity

The Holy Spirit was active throughout the history of the human race and his activity is recognized more widely through the Old Testament than is often appreciated. There are constant refer-ences in the Old Testament to his influence and involvement, and the point I wish to make in what follows is how similar this work often is to that found in the New Testament.

1. The Spirit in creation and the presence of God

In an unspecified way the Spirit was active at the time of cre-ation (Genesis 1:2), which means that at the dawning of his-tory the Spirit is seen as the executive of God or, as the Princeton theologian Benjamin Warfield expressed it, the Spirit is the immanence of the transcendent God.[6] In less theological terms, that is precisely how our Lord promised the presence of the Spirit to his disciples, as recorded in John 14:15-18, 25-26; 16:7-15.

Job thought of the Spirit as universal creator, 'By his Spirit he adorned the heavens' (Job 26:13), and Elihu had no doubt that he was also a personal creator, 'The Spirit of God has made me, and the breath of the Almighty gives me life' (Job 33:4). In fact, Elihu attributes the *sustaining* of all life to the presence of God's Spirit: 'If he should set his heart on it, if he should gather to himself his Spirit and his breath, all flesh would perish together' (Job 34:14-15); a fact that Job himself would not have disputed (Job 12:10). Psalm 104:29-30 follows exactly the same thought of the Spirit as both creator and sustainer:

> You hide your face, they are troubled;
> you take away their breath, they die
> and return to their dust.
> You send forth your Spirit, they are created.

The Spirit is also the omnipresence of God in this world: 'Where can I go from your Spirit? Or where can I flee from your presence?' (Psalm 139:7). Isaiah spoke of the Spirit as God's agent in creation who needed no direction from man: 'Who has directed the Spirit of the LORD, or as his counsellor has taught him?' (Isaiah 40:13-14).

The presence of God and his Spirit are frequently seen as equivalent; the Hebrew word translated 'presence' (*panim*) is literally 'the face' of God, and the Spirit is closely associated with this. George Montague traces the parallel between the 'face' (presence) of God and his Spirit in Exodus 33:14, for example, 'My Presence will go with you, and I will give you rest', and compares it with Isaiah 63:14, 'The Spirit of the LORD causes him to rest.' In both verses the verb 'to give rest' is identical (see also Psalm 51:11; 104:29-30; 139:7).[7] The fact that in the

Old Testament God's presence and his Spirit are inseparable is significant and reveals a more developed understanding than is often assumed.

More significant for us in this debate is the activity of the Spirit in the lives of individuals. Almost always there is a clear parallel with the same activity revealed in the New Testament. For example, it is impossible to read Genesis 4:26, 'At that time men began to call on the name of the LORD' (NIV), without realizing that we are reading of the work of the same Holy Spirit of whom the apostle writes in the New Testament, 'No one can say that Jesus is Lord except by the Holy Spirit' (1 Corinthians 12:3). This is particularly so in the light of the subsequent warning of God to the pre-Flood world that 'My Spirit shall not strive with man for ever' (Genesis 6:3).

It is surely impossible to conclude that today the human race requires the work of the Holy Spirit in order to seek after God, but that it did not need his work prior to the Flood. The Spirit may not be mentioned in the days of Seth, but he is undoubtedly there. Job saw his own existence as dependent upon the Spirit of God: 'The Spirit of God has made me, and the breath of the Almighty gives me life' (Job 33:4). And David had no doubt as to the involvement of the Spirit of God in the events of the world and in his own life: 'Where can I go from your Spirit or where can I flee from your presence?' (Psalm 139:7). It is worth comparing this with 1 Samuel 16:13: 'The Spirit of the LORD came upon David from that day forward.' *The New King James Version* is weak in translating this verse as 'The Spirit of the LORD came upon David'; the word 'came' is from a root meaning 'to rush'.

2. The Spirit for revelation

At the appointment of the seventy elders who were set apart to help Moses in leading the Israelites in the wilderness, God 'took of the Spirit that was upon him [Moses] and placed the same upon the seventy elders' (Numbers 11:25). The result was that the men prophesied. But this was not limited to the seventy, because at least two other men received the Spirit and prophesied (v. 26). There is a striking similarity between this episode and that which took place at Ephesus fifteen hundred years later. When Paul met twelve young converts to Christianity who had no knowledge of a Holy Spirit, we read, 'When Paul had laid hands on them, the Holy Spirit came upon them, and they spoke with tongues and prophesied' (Acts 19:6). Similarly, in the time of Moses, Joshua is described as 'a man in whom is the Spirit' (Numbers 27:18), just as Stephen in Acts 6:5 was described as 'a man full of faith and the Holy Spirit'. Incidentally both men were set apart through laying on of hands (compare Numbers 27:23 and Acts 6:6).

Nehemiah had no doubt that the blessing of God upon Israel in the time of Moses was because 'You also gave your good Spirit to instruct them' (Nehemiah 9:20) 'And testified against them by your Spirit in your prophets' (v. 30). This is not too dissimilar from the promise of Christ that the Spirit would convict in regard to sin, righteousness and judgement (John 16:8). Similarly the psalmist's request, 'Your Spirit is good, lead me in the land of uprightness' (Psalm 143:10), is paralleled by our Lord's promise to the disciples that the same Spirit would 'guide you into all the truth' (John 16:13).

When our Lord promised his disciples that the Spirit would 'teach you all things, and bring to your remembrance all things that I said to you' (John 14:26), there was certainly a new dynamic about his promise, but it was not a new concept. Five hundred years earlier, Nehemiah had attributed the teaching of Moses to the work of the Holy Spirit, 'You gave your good Spirit to instruct them' (Nehemiah 9:20), and so it was throughout the centuries that followed: 'For many years ... you testified against them by your Spirit in your prophets' (v. 30). Isaiah would appear to agree fully with this conclusion, and even thought of the Spirit as one who could be grieved: 'They rebelled and grieved his Holy Spirit; so he turned himself against them as an enemy, and he fought against them' (Isaiah 63:10). Not only is this an unmistakable parallel to Ephesians 4:30, 'And do not grieve the Holy Spirit of God', but it is a precise counterpart to the vigorous punishment of Ananias and Sapphira for lying to the Spirit (Acts 5:1-10). It also helps us to understand the significance of the blasphemy against the Spirit referred to in Matthew 12:31-32.[8]

None of this should be surprising. In the New Testament, Peter was aware that the Holy Spirit moved the Old Testament prophets: 'Holy men of God spoke as they were moved by the Holy Spirit' (2 Peter 1:21); but almost a millennium earlier David was aware of it also: 'The Spirit of the LORD spoke by me, and his word was on my tongue' (2 Samuel 23:2). In fact, it would seem that all the prophets were convinced of their anointing by the Spirit — see for example Ezekiel 2:2, 'The Spirit entered me', and Micah 3:8, 'I am full of power by the Spirit of the LORD.' No prophet spoke the word of the LORD without an awareness of the presence of the Spirit. For example, 'The Spirit of the LORD came upon Jahaziel' (2 Chronicles 20:14), and Zechariah paid his own tribute to 'The words which the LORD of hosts had sent by his Spirit through the former prophets' (Zechariah 7:12). Another prophet with the same name paid with his life for preaching by the Spirit: 'Then the Spirit of God came upon Zechariah son of Jehoiada the priest. He stood before the people and said, "This is what God says: 'Why do you disobey the LORD's commands? You will not prosper. Because you have forsaken the LORD, he has forsaken you.'"' (2 Chronicles 24:20, NIV). It must have been episodes like Zechariah's boldness and his subsequently being stoned that Stephen had in mind in his final condemnation of the Jews: 'You always resist the Holy Spirit; as your fathers did, so do you' (Acts 7:51). In fact, it is compelling to notice the similarity between 2 Chronicles 24:20, 'Then the Spirit of God came upon Zechariah', and Acts 7:55, 'But he [Stephen], being full of the Holy Spirit...' Sadly, the result was identical!

There is no difference between all this and Paul's conviction that 'We speak ... in words ... which the Holy Spirit teaches' (1 Corinthians 2:13), or our Lord's promise to the disciples that 'The Holy Spirit ... will bring to your remembrance all things that I said to you' (John 14:26) and 'When he, the Spirit of truth, has come, he will guide you into all the truth' (John 16:13; note that the definite article should be there before the word 'truth'). David was aware of the indwelling work of the Spirit when he cried out, 'Do not cast me away from your presence, and do not take your Holy Spirit from me' (Psalm 51:11); and Isaiah knew that his ministry came from 'The Lord God and his Spirit' (Isaiah 48:16). Sinclair Ferguson suggests that Jeremiah 1:9, 'Then the LORD put forth his hand and touched my mouth, and the LORD said to me', is in fact 'the paradigm for inspiration'. Compare this with 2 Samuel 23:2: 'The Spirit of the LORD spoke by me, and his word was on my tongue.' Consequently the New Testament writers were not creating a theology of inspiration but expounding it.

3. The Spirit and gifts for service

The first clear example of the gift of the Spirit for service comes in the help that God gave to Moses so that he did not have to bear alone the responsibility of caring for two million Israelites: 'I will take of the Spirit that is upon you and will put the same upon them' (Numbers 11:17,25). Joshua was similarly divinely aided by the Spirit in his work, and is described as 'a man in whom is the Spirit' (Numbers 27:18).

When specific work was to be done for the tabernacle, God equipped men in a way remarkably similar to the dispensing of gifts in the New Testament. To Moses, God said of Bezalel, 'I have filled him with the Spirit of God, in wisdom, in understanding, in knowledge, and in all manner of workmanship...' (Exodus 31:3; 35:31). And this was clearly not confined to one man (see Exodus 28:3). Half a millennium later the same Spirit revealed the plans of the temple to David: 'David gave his son Solomon ... the plans of all that he had [received] by the Spirit' (1 Chronicles 28:11-12). The parallel is evident in 1 Corinthians 12:4, 'There are diversities of gifts, but the same Spirit', and in verse 7, 'The manifestation of the Spirit is given to each one for the profit of all.'

The Spirit also came upon the judges of Israel: Othniel (Judges 3:10), Gideon (6:34), Jepthah (11:29), Samson (13:25; 14:19; 15:14); and upon the kings: Saul (1 Samuel 11:6) and David (16:13). He came also upon one of David's mighty warriors, Amasai (1 Chronicles12:18). Although the Spirit is not mentioned in connection with the men of Issachar whose understanding was legendary (1 Chronicles 12:32), the gift they had was surely of the same kind as the one mentioned by Paul in 1 Corinthians 12:8: 'For to one is given the word of wisdom through the Spirit, to another the word of knowledge through the same Spirit'. The same Spirit gifted both the men of Issachar and the men of Corinth.

But, like the gifts under the new covenant, the Spirit did not come upon the Old Testament servants of God with gifts for their own personal enjoyment. Their ministry was always to serve the covenant community. For this reason it is not too extravagant to observe that for those who received gifts by the Spirit in the Old Testament it was 'for the equipping of the saints for the work of ministry, for the edifying of the body of Christ' (Ephesians 4:12). The purpose then, no less than in the time of Paul, was that the people of God might be brought to unity, wisdom and Christlikeness. Warfield summarizes the work of the Spirit in the Old Testament in this way: 'He is presented as the source of all the supernatural powers and activities which are directed to the foundation and preservation and development of the Kingdom of God in the midst of the wicked world.'[9]

Under the old covenant the Spirit was equally at work in his supernatural intervention in the lives of God's servants. The powerful miracle that Philip experienced by the Spirit, which is recorded in Acts 8:39, 'The Spirit of the Lord caught Philip away...', is paralleled by that in Ezekiel 11:1, 'Then the Spirit lifted me up and brought me to the east gate of the LORD's house' (see also 3:12-15 and 1 Kings 18:12; 2 Kings 2:16).

The Puritan John Owen observed that whilst the Jews claimed that the gift of the Holy Spirit ceased after the building of the second temple in the time of Ezra and Nehemiah, they must have been referring only to prophecy, miracles and revelation since some, like Simeon and Anna (Luke 2), did receive his 'gifts and graces'. Without these, Owen comments, 'the church itself must absolutely cease.'[10]

This reference by Owen to the understanding of the Jews during the four hundred years between Malachi and Matthew, leads us to comment that whilst the rabbis considered that the Holy Spirit had departed from Israel, they nevertheless looked forward to the coming of the Messiah who would be filled with the Spirit. Meanwhile, the Spirit was considered to be a gift of God in response to obedience: 'He who undertakes a commandment in faith, is worthy that the holy spirit rest upon him.'[11] Similarly, among the Essenes (second century B.C.) the Spirit was given as the exclusive possession to those who entered the Qumran community and, in addition to wisdom, he gave forgiveness and cleansing.[12] Although this demonstrates that the Spirit was still a concept in the thinking of the Jews during the four hundred years between the Testaments, much of their understanding was false. Both the Old and New Testaments teach that the Spirit is the *cause* of obedience and membership of the community rather than a reward for entering it; though, as we shall see below, the teaching of Christ and his apostles on the subject of the Spirit did not conflict with the position generally held by the rabbis.

4. The Spirit for filling and regeneration

The phrase 'filled with the Spirit' is not confined to the post-Pentecost experience. In fact it originates in the Old Testament. This is evidenced by the fact that it is exactly this expression that is used of both Elizabeth and Zacharias (Luke 1:41,67). The workmen who were gifted by the Spirit for the construction of the tabernacle and Joshua, who took over the leadership of Israel from Moses, were each 'filled with the spirit of wisdom' (Exodus 28:3; and Deuteronomy 34:9). Of Bezalel we are specifically told that he was 'filled ... with the Spirit of God, in wisdom, in understanding, in knowledge, and in all manner of workmanship' (Exodus 31:3). Proverbs uses the idea of the spirit of wisdom being 'poured out' upon those who will turn at wisdom's rebuke (1:23). In this sense Micah claimed to be 'full of power by the Spirit of the LORD' (Micah 3:8). To be filled with the fruit of the Spirit cannot be different from being filled with the Spirit himself.

Isaiah understood something of the concept of the Spirit being 'poured [out]' as he looked forward to the new covenant (Isaiah 32:15). Similarly, Ezekiel anticipated the day when the Spirit will have been 'poured out' on the house of Israel (Ezekiel 39:29). And the prophecy of Joel 2:28 points to the time when the Spirit will be 'poured out' on all flesh. The new aspect anticipated by these last three prophets will be considered in the second part of this chapter.

On the other hand, when Isaiah 44:3 also speaks of the Spirit being poured out — the development of chapter 44 and 45 in which a new beginning is promised in the time of Cyrus — it is strongly implying that the revival of the nation at the return from exile was nothing less than an outpouring of the Spirit. If this is so, then we have a new light on that prophecy in Ezekiel 39:29 (he was preaching some two centuries later than Isaiah). Like Isaiah, he too may be referring to an outpouring at the return from exile in the year 539 B.C. This conclusion is supported by the fact that the vision of the valley of dry bones in Ezekiel 37, which is so full of the work of the Spirit, is also set in the context of the return from exile (see 39:21-29). On the prophecy in Ezekiel 39:29, Smeaton suggests, 'Perhaps it may best be regarded as a germinant prediction, having a partial or incipient accomplishment, and a full and complete accomplishment.'[13] In other words, it occurred at the return from exile, and finally at Pentecost. I am inclined to agree, and will argue later in this book for the immediate, intermediate, and ultimate fulfilment of some prophecies. From all this it is evident that not only was the concept of the pouring out or filling of the Spirit familiar to the Old Testament prophets, but they also understood it to be an experience of their own day.

What surely does not require proof is that the condition of human nature since the Fall has been the same throughout the history of the human race. When Abraham was called to serve the true and living God and abandon his pagan worship at the impressive ziggurat of the moon-god Sin in Ur of the Chaldeans, he needed a work of the Holy Spirit in his life no less than Saul of Tarsus two millennia later. That work can only be described by the New Testament word 'regeneration', a word that nowhere appears in the Old Testament. Yet to deny the need for people in the Old Testament to receive new birth by the Spirit, is to suggest that somehow Abraham of Ur was less fallen than Saul of Tarsus — or less saved! Surely the promise through Ezekiel in chapter 36:26-27, 'I will give you a new heart and put a new spirit within you; I will take the heart of stone out of your flesh and give you a heart of flesh. I will put my Spirit within you...', cannot be understood in any other way than as a reference to the new birth. In this promise of the restoration of Israel to their own land lies a description of an experience that was not altogether new to the nation, but was something that in the trauma of the exile many had forgotten.

The traditional attempt at a distinction which claims that in the Old Testament the Spirit came 'upon' men, whilst in the New he came 'into' them, simply cannot be upheld. Phrases such as 'in whom is the Spirit' (Numbers 27:18), and 'filled ... with the Spirit' (Exodus 31:3), whilst not common, are too frequent to be dismissed. I suggest that it is not wise to make a sharp distinction in the Old Testament between the use of the Hebrew prepositions *al* (meaning on, as in Numbers 11:25, NIV) and *beth* (meaning in, as in Numbers 27:18), any more than it is wise in the New Testament to make a sharp distinction between the Greek *en* (meaning in, as in John 14:17) and *epi* (meaning upon, as in Acts 1:8). It is never wise to build our theology upon prepositions. But if we do, how do we resolve the fact that the Spirit was *in* Joshua (Numbers 27:18) but that he came *on* the young disciples at Ephesus (Acts 19:6, NIV), or that God promised to put his Spirit *upon* Christ (Matthew 12:18, see also 3:16)? If we insist that after Pentecost the Spirit, who is *within* the people of God (John 14:17) comes *upon* them for particular occasions (Acts 19:6), exactly the same could be said of the Old Testament when we compare Numbers 27:18 with 11:25.

5. The Spirit for sanctification

The use of the word 'holy' to designate the Spirit, is not confined to the new covenant. Although it is not common, we find it in Psalm 51:11 and Isaiah 63:10-11. Elsewhere the psalmist acknowledges, 'Your Spirit is good. Lead me in the land of uprightness' (Psalm 143:10). It is this work in sanctifying the people of God that is most frequent in the Old Testament.

When the prophet Ezekiel condemned the nation of Israel for its rebellion against God, a rebellion which had led to the exile, he also prophesied of a day coming when Israel would be returned to its own land. This was fulfilled at the time of the decree of Cyrus, king of Persia, in 539 B.C. (Ezra 1:1-4). At the same time Ezekiel promised that Israel would return as a sanctified people:

> For I will take you out of the nations; I will gather you from all the countries and bring you back into your own land. I will sprinkle clean water on you, and you will be clean; I will cleanse you from all your impurities and from all your idols. I will give you a new heart and put a new spirit in you; I will remove from you your heart of stone and give you a heart of flesh. And I will put my Spirit in you and move you to follow my decrees and be careful to keep my laws (Ezekiel 36:24-27, NIV).

The words that he employed for this new spiritual life focused even more on the work of the Spirit than those used by Jeremiah in 31:33, when he outlined the benefits of the post-Pentecost new covenant.

Undoubtedly Jeremiah 31 is a prophecy of the new covenant. This is made clear by both its historical allusions, 'A voice was heard in Ramah, lamentation and bitter weeping, Rachel weeping for her children, refusing to be comforted for her children, because they are no more' (v. 15), and by its spiritual promises, ' "This is the covenant that I will make with the house of Israel after those days," says the LORD: "I will put my law in their minds, and write it on their hearts; and I will be their God, and they shall be my people" ' (v. 33). Yet we cannot imagine that Old Testament saints had no appreciation of the law being in their hearts — the psalmist's repeated 'I love your law' (Psalm 119:97,113,163) is evidence of this; and, as we have seen,

Ezekiel expressly promised it at the return from exile (Ezekiel 36:26-27). How widespread this was it is impossible for us to know, but clearly in those times of spiritual awakening that we will identify later in this book, there was a general delight in the law of God. This could only result from a work of the Spirit — unless we deny that all men and women are naturally rebels against God.

Sinclair Ferguson points out that 'The Spirit's ministry in the Old Testament... includes the moral ordering of the people... personal renewal of a moral and spiritual nature'. He concludes that even the fruits of the Spirit 'are already exemplified by Old Testament believers.'[14] And Smeaton comments on Proverbs 1:23, 'He means the graces of the indwelling Spirit, which were enjoyed then as well as now.'[15] For this reason the psalms are beautiful pictures of adoration and enjoyment of God with which new covenant believers can readily identify. The work of the Spirit in the Old Testament included personal transformation both morally and spiritually, hence David's plea for a 'clean heart' and a 'steadfast spirit' in the context of his fear of losing 'your Holy Spirit' (Psalm 51:10-11).

6. Symbols of the Spirit

In a small but intriguing book, Meredith Kline argues that the 'Glory-cloud' in the Old Testament — which appeared on Sinai, in the desert, over the tabernacle and at the dedication of the temple — was a reference to the active work of the Holy Spirit among his people.[16] He also sees the Spirit symbolized in the 'replica' of Aaron's vestments. These things, he claims, were not just about the reality of true redemption, but about the reality of the Holy Spirit. The oil of anointing was the climax of this: 'By this saturating anointing with the golden symbol of the Spirit of glory and life, the tabernacle vestments were impregnated with the likeness of God. In the figure of Aaron, clothed in Glory-like vestments and anointed with the holy oil, a double symbol of the Glory-Spirit stands before us.'[17] Kline goes further, and refers to the Glory-cloud that came down on the tabernacle (Exodus 40) as 'The Old Testament Pentecost event'.[18] For Kline, just as the 'Angel of the LORD' is the pre-incarnate Christ, so the Glory-cloud is the pre-Pentecost presence of the Holy Spirit.

In fact, although Kline does not draw attention to this, we may add the symbol of the lampstand in the tabernacle and temple. Of all the items made for the service of God the lampstand (Exodus 25:31-40) remained without an explanation. It was not until the vision of the prophet Zechariah, one thousand years after the original had been fashioned, that a clear explanation of its significance was given. In the fifth century B.C. Zechariah received a series of visions, one of which was of a solid gold lampstand with seven lights. It was clearly a reminder of the long since plundered lampstand of Israel's earlier days. Zechariah's vision included two olive trees which ensured a perpetual supply for the lamps. When the prophet asked the meaning of the vision he was told, ' "Not by might, nor by power, but by my Spirit," says the LORD Almighty' (Zechariah 4:1-6, NIV). Perhaps unrecognized by most, that lampstand, like the cloud and fire, had been a perpetual reminder of the presence of God by his Spirit among his people. This revelation in Zechariah was an appropriate conclusion to the old covenant, before the 'age of the Spirit' dawned.

In our laudable attempt to magnify the work of God under the new covenant, we overlook too often just how much was experienced under the old. I doubt whether the New Testament writers thought of this whole matter of discontinuity as we do. On the contrary, they were aware of the depth of spiritual experience enjoyed by their fathers in the faith. This is one reason why they quote so frequently from the Old Testament. When the disciples heard their Lord promise that he would be with

them to the very end of the age (Matthew 28:20), and when
the writer to the Hebrews drove this fact home (Hebrews 13:5),
it was by no means an entirely new concept. The phrase, 'I will
never leave you nor forsake you', finds its roots in Deuteronomy
31:6 and, as we will see elsewhere in this book, it was picked
up by Solomon who quoted it exactly in his prayer at the dedication of the temple (1 Kings 8:57). This association between
the Old and New Testaments led Smeaton to comment, 'We
find that the doctrine of the Spirit taught by the Baptist, by
Christ, and by the apostles, was in every respect the same as
that with which the Old Testament church was familiar. We nowhere find that their Jewish hearers on any occasion took exception to it. The teaching of our Lord and his apostles on this
topic never called forth a question or an opposition from any
quarter...'[19]

Just as we must be allowed to speak of justification, regeneration, sanctification and even being filled with the Spirit as true
experiences for the men and women of faith in the Old Testament, so we can speak of revival. I would go further than
Meredith Kline who claims that the Glory-cloud that appeared
over the tabernacle in Exodus 40 was 'The Old Testament version of Pentecost'. Just as the appearances of the 'Angel of the
LORD' were 'pre-Incarnation incarnations', and every sacrifice
in Israel was a 'pre-Calvary calvary', so the Glory-cloud was a
'pre-Pentecost pentecost'. In each case, the value of the symbol
was the same as the ultimate reality itself; though the revelation
was not so full nor the effect so powerful and wide-ranging as
that which took place at Pentecost. To this we must now turn.

Holy Spirit and Pentecost — discontinuity

Having emphasized the continuity of the work of the Spirit, it
might appear that a case has been made that there is absolutely
no difference in the work of the Spirit between the two

covenants! Warfield goes so far as to claim, 'In passing from the Old Testament to the New, the reader is conscious of no violent discontinuity in the conception of the Spirit which he finds in the two volumes.' [20] On the other hand, whilst recognizing that the Spirit's activity in the Old Testament involved personal renewal of a moral and spiritual nature, Sinclair Ferguson is right to insist that 'Any biblical theology of the Spirit's work must recognize the progressive and cumulative character of historical revelation', and to warn that recognizing the deep-rooted continuity of his work can lead us into the danger of 'flattening the contours of redemptive history, and of undermining the genuine diversity and development from the old to new covenants'. [21]

That there is a new era of the work of the Spirit with the coming of the Messiah is evident, if only because of John 7:39, 'Whom those believing in him would receive; for the Holy Spirit was not yet given, because Jesus was not yet glorified.' The context here, as we shall see, is world mission. God's revelation of the work of the Spirit, just as his revelation of the work of redemption and of his own character, reaches its fulfilment in Jesus Christ. The emphasis in this verse, which is often misunderstood, is not to look back to the old covenant where clearly the Spirit had been given to the church, but to look forward to the experience promised in Acts 1:4-5.

1. Revelation — a clearer understanding

There seems little doubt that whilst the Holy Spirit was active throughout the Old Testament: in creation, regeneration, equipping and supplying gifts for service, in the revelation of Scripture and prophesy, and in revival, there was a significant lack of understanding of the person and work of the Spirit. In the progressive revelation through the Old Testament we can learn more at each stage of history, but we could never formulate a full doctrine of the person and work of the Spirit from the Old

Testament alone. George Smeaton extravagantly claimed that
'Isaiah has scattered through his prophecies allusions to the
Sprit so manifold and various, in express descriptions and in
brief turns of phrase, that it might not be difficult to put together, from his words, the complete doctrine of the Spirit.'[22]
Warfield at first quotes Smeaton approvingly,[23] although his
unqualified support was apparently too hasty, since he later
admits that there are aspects of the person and work of the
Spirit that require the revelation of the New Testament.[24] There
is no reference to the Spirit of God in at least half the books of
the Old Testament, and in the entire fifty-two chapters of the
prophet Jeremiah, the Spirit is not directly referred to once.
Significantly, when Jeremiah expounds on the new covenant in
glowing language (31:31-34) he does not explicitly cast it in
terms of the Spirit, even though Paul distinctly claims that the
new covenant is a covenant of the Spirit (2 Corinthians 3:6).
Clearly then, God did not reveal all his secrets even to his
prophets. Warfield expresses the same thing in this way, 'What
is most fundamental in the biblical doctrine of the Spirit of God
is common to both testaments... But it is not equally common
in all parts of the Bible... It is found as often in the epistles of
Paul as in the whole Old Testament.'[25]

James Montgomery Boice admitted that in the Old Testament there are 'intimations of the doctrine of the distinct personality of the Holy Spirit' and he continued, 'It must be admitted
that in the Old Testament there is very little in the way of clear
presentation of the personal distinctness of the second person
of the Trinity and even less of the personal distinctness of the
Spirit of God.'[26] In short, the men of Issachar may have had
little, if any, knowledge of where their ability came from, whereas
the men of Corinth most certainly did.

When Paul met the new Christian converts in Ephesus and
asked them if they had received the Holy Spirit when they believed (Acts 19:2), I doubt very much whether their response

confused him as much as it seems to have confused generations of commentators. Their reply, 'We have not so much as heard whether there is a Holy Spirit', was not surprising on two counts. In the first place, if they were Gentile converts, there was little in their religious background to prepare them for such a theology. In the second place, they appear to have been led to Christ by a disciple of John the Baptist, who apparently reflected the limited understanding of the work of the Spirit in the Old Testament; though the Baptist himself understood more, as John 1:32-33 reveals. In fact, their reply could have been reproduced by many of the Old Testament saints. This is hardly surprising when we recall that little was written by the Jews about the Holy Spirit during the almost half a millennium from Malachi to Matthew. Although the Qumran scrolls, which date from this period, do refer to the Spirit, they reveal no doctrine of a personal Spirit and they contain no equivalent word for the wonderful New Testament word 'paraclete'.

In the light of this, what did Jesus mean when Nicodemus expressed his confusion over the subject of the new birth? Our Lord's response, 'Are you the teacher of Israel, and do not know these things?' (John 3:10), may imply that he expected Nicodemus to understand. If this was so, we may wonder just how much understanding of regeneration anyone would be expected to gain from the Old Testament alone. We may read new birth into the comment 'God changed Saul's heart'(1 Samuel 10:9, NIV; literally, 'turned him a new heart') — or we may not! But that is our post-Pentecost advantage. Perhaps Nicodemus ought to have understood the deep significance of Ezekiel 36:26-27: 'I will give you a new heart and put a new spirit within you; I will take the heart of stone out of your flesh and give you a heart of flesh. I will put my Spirit within you...' On the other hand, could there be a note of sarcasm in our Lord's response to Nicodemus? But that would be out of order, since Nicodemus was not an aggressive questioner but a sincere enquirer. The only other conclusion must be that our Lord was challenging this teacher to be ready for a deeper under-standing of the work of the Spirit than he had ever been aware of. Teacher of Israel he may be, but the day had arrived when all the Lord's people would understand more than he did. The question was therefore rhetorical; it was designed to draw the enquirer's enquiry even further.

This is not to say that some of the prophets were not given significant insight into the future glory of the coming of the Spirit at Pentecost and beyond. The expression, 'I will pour out my Spirit', occurs only occasionally (Isaiah 44:3; Ezekiel 39:29; Joel 2:28-29; and possibly Proverbs 1:23), but Donald Guthrie makes some helpful comments on three of the major Old Testament expectations of the coming Spirit.[27] On Ezekiel 37 he writes, 'Its massive extent prepares us for the corporate outpouring of the Spirit at Pentecost.' On Isaiah 44:3 he says, 'Here the outpouring is wider, since it is not confined to the house of Israel.' And on Joel 2:28 he comments, 'This is particularly significant because it shows that the mass descent of the Spirit was not without prior preparation.' Guthrie takes us further, and enquires why there is such a lack of teaching on the Holy Spirit in the first three Gospels. His conclusion is, 'Because it required the experi-ence of Pentecost to make the teaching intelligible'.[28] The same, of course, could be said of the whole of the Old Testament.

2. Experience — a personal relationship

To limit the significance of Pentecost to a new revelation or understanding of the work of the Spirit, however significant that might be, would be a relatively sterile conclusion in the light of the massive events that we read about in Acts and the Epistles. A hallmark of the new covenant is that it is 'not of the letter but of the Spirit' (2 Corinthians 3:6). When John the Bap-tist introduced the Messiah as 'he whom God has sent' and added that to him 'God does not give the Spirit by measure' (John 3:34), there is more than a hint that up until this point God's Spirit had been given with constraint. It is in this way that we must surely understand John 7:39: 'Up to that time the Spirit had not been given, since Jesus had not yet been glorified' (NIV). When Jesus breathed on his disciples and declared, 'Receive the Holy Spirit' (John 20:22), this was a symbolic act pointing to the forthcoming Pentecost. It is certain that these men were regenerate already and that the Spirit therefore indwelt them; what our Lord was now seeking to do was to prepare them for a greater experience of initiation — but what, exactly, was this new experience?

When Christ instructed his disciples concerning the work of the Spirit in the individual — convicting of sin, righteousness and judgement (John 16:8) — this was more than simply drawing back the veil on what the Spirit's work had always been. Certainly the Spirit had been active in the lives of individuals in conviction and conversion; if he had not, no one would have been saved since the Fall. But the disciples would experience something more. The fulfilment of the promise in Jeremiah 31:34, ' "No more shall every man teach his neighbour, and every man his brother, saying, 'Know the LORD,' for they shall all know me, from the least of them to the greatest of them," says the LORD', is to be found in the promise of our Lord that the Spirit would be known as the 'paraclete' or counsellor. From now on every disciple of Christ could understand the Scriptures for himself. Calvin, in his commentary on Jeremiah, makes some wise observations on this, taking it to be a hyperbole of the new understanding that the Spirit gives under the new covenant; thus, he concludes, it does not negate the need for teachers. Let me explore this a little more since it is very important but easily misunderstood.

John Calvin, whilst convinced that Old Testament saints were truly regenerate and could enjoy the law of God, confronts the question of what a passage like this in Jeremiah really means. His conclusion is that the power of the law to penetrate the heart was not inherent in the law itself, but was 'transferred to the law from the gospel'. In other words, God's grace allowed them to experience the law as if they were under the new covenant. There is, of course, nothing novel in this concept since David himself experienced forgiveness for a sin which could not be atoned for under the law (2 Samuel 12:13; compare Leviticus 20:10). Pentecost provided such an outpouring of the Spirit that *all* new covenant believers can experience the reality of God's Word in a way that only a few did under the old covenant.

But there is more to the new experience of Pentecost than this. The Old Testament saint saw himself chiefly in the community of the people of God who belonged to the land of Israel; there was no other way for him to view Judaism. The nationhood of Israel was as much associated with the land as it was associated with their covenant with God; the two were inseparable. Church and state, geography and nationhood were indistinguishable. This is part of the reason why exile, an unfamiliar concept to modern-day Christians who often make their home far from their land of birth, was such a terrible judgement for the Jews. The concept of a believer on his own would have been very difficult for the Israelite to grasp. For this reason the psalmist focuses so much on the city (Psalm 48, for example) and the temple (Psalm 84, for example). His own spiritual life was first and foremost within that context, and to be denied either was a significant spiritual loss. Of course, it was not impossible for the Old Testament to conceive of a spiritual life separated from the nation of Israel, but the examples of Naaman (2 Kings 5), and Nineveh (Jonah 3) are exceptional.

Worship centred on a fixed place in Jerusalem at the tabernacle or temple. This is the central theme of Psalm 42:4 and Psalm 84, where, in each instance the psalmist felt a deep sense of loss because he was unable to meet at the tabernacle or temple. Spurgeon refers to the psalmist's 'holy love-sickness' for the temple. It was mandatory for the men to attend the temple three times each year (Deuteronomy 16:16) and for this reason Daniel, in exile, prayed towards Jerusalem (Daniel 6:10). Even when the nation was taken into exile, wherever Israel found itself, it was the Scriptures and the synagogue that held the community of faith together. During the life of Christ, he and his disciples regularly worshipped at the temple. Although wise saints of the old covenant knew that a building could not confine the eternal Creator (1 Kings 8:27), nevertheless the temple represented God dwelling among his people.

Pentecost changed all this and the temple very soon became wholly irrelevant to the Christian community. Part of the symbol of the tongues of fire was that God now dwelt within all disciples of Christ so that each became a temple of the Spirit (1 Corinthians 6:19), and together they are built into a holy temple (Ephesians 2:21-22). Throughout the Old Testament these two concepts awaited their fulfilment at Pentecost. From now on the visible symbols of the presence of God among his people Israel — the cloud, temple, theophany — would be gone for ever, and the invisible, indwelling Holy Spirit would be the presence of Christ among his people. This is exactly the major significance of our Lord's teaching in John 14 - 16.

But more than this, Pentecost brought a gospel for the whole world, and that essential community consciousness, though still important in the concept of 'the church', was no longer the *essence* of the faith. The Christian life is certainly not national or even primarily communal; the church-state link has been, or should be, for ever broken. The *essence* of the gospel is now personal. For this reason it was possible, and would become common, for Christians to live out their faith in the far-flung corners of the Roman Empire — and beyond — even if there were no other Christians around. The new covenant people needed no physical temple, synagogue or even community (*ecclesia*) to maintain their faith. Valuable though the latter was it was not *essential* to spiritual life. None of this denies the possibility of an enjoyment of a personal relationship with God by old covenant saints — the Psalms and Job 29:4 alone prove how rich this could be — but Pentecost introduced an era when such an intimate relationship would be commonplace among *all* who were regenerate.

The new covenant experience of the Spirit taught adoption as a personal experience and not as a national association. This was not altogether absent from the Old Testament (see, for example, Jeremiah 3:4) but it was little known. Paul introduced a radically new emphasis in Romans 8:14-16 (NIV), when he wrote, 'Those who are led by the Spirit of God are sons of God. For you did not receive a spirit that makes you a slave again to fear, but you received the Spirit of sonship. And by him we cry, "*Abba*, Father." The Spirit himself testifies with our spirit that we are God's children.' Under the old covenant, adoption was because of membership of the community of Israel; under the new covenant the position is reversed and membership of the new Israel (the church) is because of adoption by God. Next to justification, adoption is a central privilege of the Christian gospel.

The Glory-cloud of which Meredith Kline writes is no longer to be thought of as hovering over the tabernacle or even the congregation, but entering the individual. If we follow this symbolism, our attention will turn to 'the tongues of fire' that came to rest on each of the disciples at Pentecost. The significance of this is that the pillar of fire, symbolizing the presence of God among his people, is no longer only over the community but within each believer. The *New International Version*, perhaps, captures the significance of the word 'divided' that describes the tongues of fire: 'They saw what seemed to be tongues of fire that separated and came to rest on each of them' (Acts 2:3).

None of this denies the importance of the community found in the Christian congregation. This is a theme that Paul emphasizes constantly, not least in his letter to the Ephesians where he frequently employs words beginning with the Greek preposition *sun*, meaning 'together with' — it is found three times in chapter 3:6, for example. In case it should be thought that I am minimizing the significance of the New Testament stress upon the value of the church as community, it may be helpful to show just how often Paul, in Ephesians, uses words beginning with the prefix *sun* with reference to the Christian community: made alive together (2:5); raised up together, seated together (2:6); fitted together (2:21); built together (2:22); heirs together, members together, sharers together (3:6, NIV); together with all the saints (3:18, NIV); (literally) bound together (4:3); joined together and knit together (4:16). In some respects the New Testament presents the concept of community as even more important than under the old covenant, but it is less essential. Significant it may be, but it is not of the essence of spiritual life.

Nor does this position deny the presence of the Spirit over a community — which is often experienced particularly in revival. But it lays the focus elsewhere — in the life of the individual. Today, Western Christianity is sometimes accused of ignoring the biblical significance of community; that may be true, but we must not return to the Old Testament concept that community is all. The Spirit came to make the experience of individual faith very real. That is a significant shift between the two testaments.

In the Old Testament the experience of Bezalel and the men of Issachar was exceptional; now, however, 'The manifestation of the Spirit is given to each one for the profit of all' (1 Corinthians 12:7). Gifts are given by the personal intervention of the Holy Spirit to all the Lord's people, not simply to a select few. Undoubtedly the gifts are to be used for the common good; and the interdependence of believers cannot be doubted

either (no one can say, 'I have no need of you' 1 Corinthians
12:21), but the significant new factor is that 'each one' receives
a spiritual gift.

In addition, the concepts of 'being filled with the Spirit' and
of being 'baptized in the Spirit' clearly have a new dynamic
under the new covenant. We have already seen that the presence of the Spirit coming powerfully upon men in the Old Testament is not entirely absent. However, it was not commonplace,
and even the vision that was given to Ezekiel in the valley of
bones, together with the promise, 'I will put my Spirit in you,
and you shall live' (Ezekiel 37:14), was directed to the corporate life of Israel. In the New Testament the entire company of
Christians was filled with the Spirit repeatedly and individually
(e.g. Acts 4:31).

3. Ministry — a universal commission

Another significant mark of the discontinuity of the work of the
Spirit between the two covenants must be the result of his outpouring at Pentecost. Since that time, every true believer is privil-
eged to act as prophet and priest, and this is not simply by
virtue of the nature of redemption completed by Christ at
Calvary, but through the indwelling Holy Spirit. When the Holy
Spirit came down upon the Christians at Pentecost they could
now return to the furthest parts of the Roman Empire and worship God without the need of a priest as intermediary. But just
as important, they all became prophets to the nations, commis-
sioned and anointed to achieve what only a few prophets had
been allowed to do through the centuries of the Old Testament.

Commenting on Zechariah 4 and comparing it with Revelation 1 and 11, Meredith Kline concludes, 'The message of the
church is that the covenant people will be empowered by God's
Spirit, symbolized by the oil, to accomplish its prophetic light-
bearing witness to the world.'[29] Elsewhere Kline concludes that
Pentecost is the 'entrée into the councils that had been the

peculiar privilege of prophets and apostles caught up in the
Spirit. It is now the normal task of everyone, and so the longing
of Moses is fulfilled: all the Lord's people are prophets — in the
Spirit.'[30] This reference to Numbers 11:29 is significant. After
Pentecost all Christians are to carry the message of God to the
nations. Until now only the prophets had been expected to be
ambassadors for Judaism. Now, however, merchants, civil servants and soldiers are emissaries for the gospel of Jesus Christ
— all the Lord's people are prophets.

James Jordan looks at this in a similar way. Following on
the work of Kline he suggests that the prophets were members
of 'God's Divine Council', a privilege that was lost to mankind
at the Fall. From then on only a few — that is, the prophets —
were reinstated to this privilege. Examples of reinstatement to
this position are found in Genesis 18:17, 'Shall I hide from
Abraham what I am doing...?', and Numbers 12:6-8, 'I speak
with him face to face.' However, Jordan concludes that under
the new covenant, 'Everyone would be made full-time council
members.'[31] He does not tell us how, but surely it must be through
the knowledge of the full and final revelation in Christ and his
Word.

The fulfilment of Joel 2 claimed by Peter in Acts 2 is more
than significant — it is literally world changing:

And afterwards, I will pour out my Spirit on all people.
Your sons and daughters will prophesy, your old men will
dream dreams, your young men will see visions. Even on
my servants, both men and women, I will pour out my
Spirit in those days, and they will prophesy... And everyone who calls on the name of the LORD will be saved
(Acts 2:18,21, quoting Joel 2:28-29,32, NIV).

The vital part of Joel's promise is the point at which Peter stops
in his quotation. Too often the focus is upon the prophecy,
dreams and visions, but they are only means to an end, and

the end is that 'Whoever calls on the name of the LORD shall be saved.' This is the point at which the covenant of God assumes a universal offer. The 'whoever' is clarified by Paul in Romans 10:12-13 (NIV) where, quoting this same verse from Joel 2:32, he insists that 'There is no difference between Jew and Gentile.'

What the Spirit now accomplishes is the creation of an army of new-covenant men and women who, as members of the divine council, can understand more fully than was ever possible before, God's gracious plans for people from 'All nations, tribes, peoples and tongue' (Revelation 7:9). Prophecy — telling God's message — is no longer the preserve of a few but the privilege of all. The tongues of fire symbolized the pouring out of the Spirit in the lives of men and women from every part of the Roman Empire and beyond. But the gift of speaking in these very languages (tongues) was God's seal that he was sending his message to the whole world and that all his people were now prophets in the sense of proclaiming the message without distinction of Jew or Gentile.

The exclusivism of Israel had become such that by the time of Christ even Proselytes (believing Gentiles) were segregated at meals; this is what made some of his associations so shocking. In this sense the 'Samaritan pentecost' (Acts 8:14-17) and the 'Gentile pentecost' (Acts 10:44-46; compare Peter's comment in 11:15: 'The Holy Spirit fell upon them, as upon us at the beginning.') were even more radical events than the Jewish Pentecost. Nothing like this had happened since the days of Jonah — and even that was a passing phenomenon. This was now to be permanent.

When our Lord told his disciples that 'It has been given to you to know the mysteries of the kingdom of heaven' (Matthew 13:11), he was saying much more than that they alone would be able to understand the parables. They were now becoming full-time prophets with a commission to evangelize the whole world. This was a major secret of the kingdom of heaven that was never fully revealed until Pentecost. Similarly, when our

Lord promised that 'out of [the] heart [of all who come to him] will flow rivers of living water' (John 7:38), it was far more than a promise of personal fulfilment and private enjoyment; it was a coded claim that when the Holy Spirit came there would be a massive outflow of 'living water' (the gospel) from all who had slaked their own spiritual thirst at the well of salvation. That was a reference to mission.

Something was happening in Acts 2:8-11 that Moses, even in his wildest hopes, could hardly have expected as an answer to his longing that all the Lord's people would be prophets and that 'The LORD would put his Spirit upon them' (Numbers 11:29). Jewish pilgrims from what would be known today as Iran, Iraq, Syria, Palestine, Turkey, Armenia, Egypt, Libya, Italy, Crete, Jordan and Lebanon returned to their homes filled with the Spirit, to declare 'the wonders of God'. No longer were they God-fearing Jews 'from every nation under heaven' (Acts 2:5) jealously guarding the faith in their synagogues, they were now disciples of Christ with a world-wide evangelistic mission. By the end of Acts 8 Ethiopia had been added to the list. This prophetic ministry was now the task of every believer. A new era of the Spirit's work had dawned.

4. Power — a prophetic authority

Our Lord promised his disciples that they would receive 'power when the Holy Spirit comes on you' (Acts 1:8, NIV). This was the opening of a new chapter in the work of the Spirit, and it would enable them to fulfil their new commission. The promise of power was not only for a flurry of miracles that would prove to be 'signs of an apostle' (2 Corinthians 12:12), nor even for the incredible — but rarely repeated — gift of speaking in un-known languages as recorded in Acts 2, 10 and 19. The real evidence of the power of the Spirit is located in the authority of God's Word and the testimony of changed lives. This must be so in the light of the Bible and history. It is evident to the most casual reader that over the succeeding two millennia the church has grown, not through what are commonly called 'miracles and wonders', but through the Spirit working through the Word of God and the transformed lives of those converted to Christ.

This is precisely what we would expect from the New Testament. Paul placed all his confidence in 'a demonstration of the Sprit's power', which he defined as 'My speech and my preaching' (1 Corinthians 2:4). In consequence of this, lives were changed and Paul could commend the Corinthians for the fact that 'You are our epistle written in our hearts, known and read by all men; clearly you are an epistle of Christ, ministered by us, written not with ink but with the Spirit of the living God, not on tablets of stone but on tablets of flesh, that is, of the heart' (2 Corinthians 3:2). The nearest approach to this found in the Old Testament is in the promise of Ezekiel 36:26-27 and in God's insistence that the Israelites should keep all his laws so that the surrounding nations would conclude, 'Surely this great nation is a wise and understanding people' (Deuteronomy 4:5-8). But, once again, the emphasis there is upon national, rather than individual, responsibility. Of course the latter was necessary, but it was the corporate witness that was primarily in focus under the old covenant. The New Testament focus is always upon the transformation of the individual so that the corporate witness of the church will be effective. And it is always in that order.

The 'greater works' promised by our Lord to all who believe in him (John 14:12) have been manipulated too often to a false end. If seen as a reference solely to the miracles worked by Christ then the promise has patently failed. No individual has ever equalled, let alone exceeded, the miracles of Christ. How could they? The whole purpose of the supernatural in our Lord's life was to demonstrate his divine authority as the Son of God (John 14:11). However, the greatest thing that he had been doing was preaching the Kingdom of God to 'the lost sheep of the house of Israel' (Matthew 15:24). On his own admission he had been sent to these alone. In John 14 the disciples were promised that all who have faith in him will do far greater things; and this refers to the universal mission of the church after Pentecost. In the context of John 14, our Lord immediately went on to give his disciples the most detailed teaching on the promised coming of the Spirit that they would ever receive (John 14 - 17). Significantly perhaps, from here until the resurrection there is not one reference to, or example of, a miracle.

The promise by our Lord of the gift of the Spirit to the disciples was more often than not in the context of their new commission. Thus the 'Counsellor' will be sent to the disciples so that the world will be convinced of sin, righteousness and judgement (John 16:8). Similarly, when Christ breathed on the disciples and said, 'Receive the Holy Spirit' (John 20:22), he immediately placed this action in the context of their ministry of reconciling sinners to God. The same, of course, is true in Acts 1:8. All of this authority, both through the Word and by the life, is available no longer to the favoured few members of what James Jordan calls 'The Divine Council', but to all who are disciples of Christ. In this sense it is an unlimited outpouring of the Spirit. The power of the Spirit is given to the disciples of Christ so that they might exercise, not only the prophetic ministry, but the same prophetic authority of the elite few under the old covenant. The gospel, through the Spirit, is the power of God for salvation to everyone who believes, and every Christian carries that authority.

Conclusion

Here then are the key elements in the difference between the Spirit working before and after Pentecost. Before Pentecost every man and woman of faith was indwelt by the Spirit for their new birth and their new life; this much has to be accepted or else, as we have said, we must demonstrate why and how human nature, and therefore salvation, was different then. This same Holy Spirit would give faith, and make God and his law real. Only by the Spirit could the psalmist exclaim, 'Oh, how I love your law!' (Psalm 119:97). I believe that those special periods of spiritual awakening, times of revival, were also evidence of the powerful work of the Spirit of God. What then is the difference pre and post Pentecost? Firstly, his person and work are *more fully understood* after Pentecost. Secondly, his activity is *more personal as an experience*; the pillar of fire over the nation of Israel becomes the indwelling Spirit for believers from all nations on earth. Thirdly, his work is *massively evangelistic* in its results, sending every recipient of the Spirit on the errand of universal mission. And fourthly the disciples of Christ receive a *new power and authority* for the fulfilment of their great commission.

None of this was entirely unknown throughout the Old Testament, but all of it was merely embryonic there; a select few understood and/or experienced it more or less. Those pre-Pentecost pentecosts that I do not hesitate to call revival were, like so much of the Old Testament, a foreshadowing of the better things that were to come. However, unlike the sacrifices, which had no value in themselves and could offer salvation only in the light of the cross of Christ, the Spirit's work was effective in its own right. Though both the sacrifices and revival anticipated the greater and final revelation that was to come.

From what has been said, it should be clear that the emphasis upon the outpouring, or filling or baptism of the Spirit under the new covenant has nothing to do with receiving a greater proportion of the Spirit than was possible under the old covenant. The idea of the Spirit coming to the elect in percentage points is biblically and theologically inept. For this reason, words like 'degree' and 'measure' are perhaps unhelpful in this discussion. It is not the quantity of the Spirit that is in focus nor even, primarily, the quality of his work, but the manner and purpose of his coming and its results. Regeneration is a new birth whether under the old covenant or the new, and one consequence is a transformed life. In the same way, under whichever covenant it is effected, justification is an absolving of guilt, one consequence of which is reconciliation to God.

I therefore do not believe that the difference between revival in the Old Testament and the period of the New Testament church is one of kind and quality or, strictly speaking, of degree and measure. Rather, it is a matter of extent and purpose. The word I would prefer to use is 'potential'. That word carries the idea of a capability or purpose that is latent, waiting for the fullness of time before being fully unleashed. In other words, the Spirit gave himself fully to his people in the Old Testament, but with a more limited purpose in view, and therefore with a greater restraint. As a consequence, whilst there was undoubtedly personal revival in, for example, the time of Hezekiah (we will see in chapter 3 that revival is always a people's movement), it did not have all the wider marks of New Testament revival.

Under the old covenant the Spirit was at work both in the individual and in the community. The marks of his activity, which resembled his post-Pentecost work, can be seen clearly in the light of our new covenant insight. In consequence of this, conviction, regeneration and revival are all appropriate words for the work of the Spirit in the Old Testament. However, he limited his potential until the time had fully come, and at Pentecost he came upon the people of God in a universal outpouring for a universal purpose, so that with a new understanding, experience, commission and authority they might win the world for Christ.

2.
Examples of revival in the Old Testament

In the previous chapter we confronted the idea that nothing before Pentecost can properly be called a revival unless we 'undermine the genuine diversity and development from old to new covenants'. In answering this challenge we established both the continuity and diversity of the work of the Spirit in the old and new covenants, before and after Pentecost. No one would suggest that in the Old Testament we will discover all that there is to know about any Christian doctrine; there is more light and more understanding in the progressive revelation of God through the Old Testament and into the New. Job surely understood something of a future life with God beyond the grave — his outburst recorded in Job 19:25-27 reveals this — but we would not expect to learn all that we can know about heaven from the Book of Job. However, to assert that we cannot speak of Job's eternal hope without undermining the genuine diversity and development from old to new covenants would be to set up an unjustified barrier against Old Testament study.

I similarly believe that wherever we discover a significant spiritual 'awakening' among God's covenant people in the Old Testament, we can speak of it as revival. In the same way we can refer to Abraham, Moses and David as men who had experienced regeneration and were justified through faith alone. We have already seen that in Romans 4 Paul uses Abraham as his *example* of faith and not simply as an illustration. He refers also to the 'Christian' faith of Moses in Hebrews 11:26. When

Paul informed the Christians at Rome that 'everything that was written in the past was written to teach us' (Romans 15:4, NIV) he surely implied that on every subject it deals with, there is something we can learn from the Old Testament.

The study of revival is no different, unless we have decided in advance that this subject is a peculiarly new-covenant experience. This is the position that Iain Murray maintains when he writes, 'While the phenomenon of revival certainly exists in Old Testament *prophecy* we cannot introduce the *experience* into the Old Testament without seriously affecting its meaning. Of course there are important lessons to be drawn from God's mighty acts in the Old Testament era but when these are made the basis for interpreting the New Testament teaching we are bound to go wrong' (italics original).[1] He is right to warn against interpreting the New Testament by the Old, but I am not doing this. On the contrary, I wish to show that on some issues there is a steady development and increasing revelation throughout the Old Testament into the New. Just as we can discover the experience of regeneration in the Old Testament by our fuller knowledge of it from the New, so I tried to show in chapter 1 that we can understand the work of the Holy Spirit in the Old Testament by a comparison and contrast with his work in the New.

In the next four chapters I shall seek to demonstrate that in the Old Testament God periodically sent his Holy Spirit to revive his people from a time of spiritual decline or disobedience, with the result that they enjoyed a renewed relationship with him. I want to show also that many of the hallmarks of what has been called 'revival' throughout the age of the church, were evident in these Old Testament experiences, and that the Old Testament prophets came to think of their God as a revival-giving God. The experience of none of them was identical to that of Pentecost, but the expectation of many of them was. The remainder of this chapter is simply an overview.

From Creation to the Exodus

Throughout the story of God's people in the Old Testament there is a constant cycle of spiritual decline and spiritual revival both personally and nationally. The first indication of spiritual revival is to be found in Genesis 4:26 with the remarkable statement, 'Then men began to call on the name of the LORD.' I am aware that commentators have disagreed as to exactly what happened at this time, and we cannot know for certain. However, whatever the verse means, it clearly implies that from the fall of Adam onwards there was a steady decline until the position had been reached where his descendants were no longer calling upon God. This is more than hinted at in the actions of both Cain and Lamech (Genesis 4:16,23-24). For one hundred and thirty years the consequences of the Fall spiralled downwards until Seth was born (v. 25).

It is possibly significant that Seth's son was named 'Enosh'; that name comes from a verb meaning 'to be weak or frail' (though not all agree with this derivation of the Hebrew word). If it refers to Seth's recognition of the physical mortality and spiritual frailty of human nature in contrast to the nature of God, then Seth stands in marked contrast to the prevailing and violent arrogance of Lamech and the descendants of Cain (Genesis 4:23-24). The Hebrew scholar Keil undoubtedly came close to the reality when he commented, 'While the family of the Cainites, by the erection of a city and the invention and development of worldly arts and business, were laying the foundation for the kingdom of this world, the family of the Sethites began, by united invocation of the name of the God of grace, to found and erect the Kingdom of God.'[2]

Perhaps we cannot assume that no one prayed before Seth, but it is generally accepted that the form of the Hebrew strongly implies that from this time on men used the name of the LORD (Yahweh) in worship. This would therefore be the first notice in

Scripture that the character of God as the LORD was recognized and worshipped by fallen humanity. It is a matter of debate how far Seth and his family used the covenant name of God simply as the means of access to him and how far they understood the character of God that was revealed in that name (see Exodus 3:13-15, and 6:2-4). However, what is clear is that a radical turning point in the division of the human race had begun.

Many commentators see this as the commencement of public worship, as opposed to the private worship of God.[3] Calvin goes so far as to suggest that at this point in history, 'The face of the church began distinctly to appear.' He even compares it to the events of his own day: 'Such a restoration of religion has been effected also in our time' (the sixteenth century). Whether or not this is pressing the account too far, it is clear that from this time on, some people publicly called on the true God and some, perhaps most, did not. If we hold a correct view of the fallenness of human nature and of the necessity of the work of the Holy Spirit in regeneration, then this shift can be explained only in terms of a new and powerful work of God by his Spirit. Anything less does scant justice to the importance of this verse in Scripture. The effect of that spiritual revival was decisive for the future of the human race. Noah, from the line of Seth, was a descendant of revival and he and his family alone survived the universal Flood.

From the Flood to the years of the Patriarchs we are following the story of one family through Abraham, Isaac and Jacob. The spiritual focus is narrowed to the lives of these men, and little is known of the religious commitment of their families or of the wider circle of their servants. All three men knew periods of backsliding: Abraham in Egypt, Isaac in Gerar, and Jacob towards the end of his stay in Padan Aram. Abraham and Jacob also knew times of spiritual renewal. Abraham experienced a remarkable interview with God when his sacrifice was miraculously burned up (Genesis 15), and Jacob's great spiritual experience took place at the River Jabbok, where he wrestled with the man of God and determined, 'I will not let you go unless you bless me!' (Genesis 32). Each of these episodes describes their struggle with God until blessing and assurance came. But to use the word 'revival' to describe them may be a definition too far. In the experience of the Patriarchs there would appear to have been nothing approaching an outpouring of spiritual life that greatly affected those around them. Ron Davies correctly reminds us that 'Times of reformation and covenant renewal were not necessarily times of spiritual revival.'[4]

For more than four hundred years the descendants of Jacob, or Israel as we know them, suffered in Egypt. During this time their spiritual life was undoubtedly affected, as may be evidenced by their eager return to the idols of Egypt (Exodus 32). In the Book of Exodus we are introduced to a cycle of events with which we become familiar throughout the Old Testament. A summary is found in Exodus 2:23-25:

> During that long period, the king of Egypt died. The Israelites groaned in their slavery and cried out, and their cry for help because of their slavery went up to God. God heard their groaning and he remembered his covenant with Abraham, with Isaac and with Jacob. So God looked on the Israelites and was concerned about them (NIV).

They were in a desperate situation, and had been for four hundred years. They cried out for help, and the compassion of God in answering them was based upon his covenant promises and his active intervention in the past. It is hard to describe what followed as anything other than a spiritual revival in the Old Testament sense.

From Sinai to the Judges

The story of the Exodus and the giving of the law on Mount Sinai is well known. But what is often overlooked is that it represents a spiritual resurrection for the people of Israel. Not even the disastrous episode of the golden calf can interfere with the fact that what happened to the people at the Exodus and at Sinai was an incredible spiritual revival. For four hundred years they had been in spiritual decline and out of desperation they cried to God. He set them free from their slavery, brought them into the wilderness to Mount Sinai, shook the mountain with thunder, lightning 'and a very loud trumpet blast' (NIV), and gave them his laws. To suggest that their united commitment, 'All the words which the LORD has said we will do' (Exodus 24:3,7), was nothing more than a terrified response to the awesome presence of God is surely to downgrade what God was doing among his people. In spite of their apostasy in little over a month (Exodus 32), God was at work in the hearts of his people; they meant what they said and this was a spiritual revival.

To deny this leaves us with the alternative that, in the Old Testament, God only ever motivated his people by fear and never by faith. Fear alone may possibly fit the story after the awesome events of Sinai, but even before those events we read, 'Then all the people answered together and said, "All that the LORD has spoken we will do" ' (Exodus 19:8). This full-hearted response was surely not merely a reaction of fear. If we may project more than six hundred years beyond Sinai, fear is certainly not an explanation for the promise of God to Solomon in 2 Chronicles 7:14. Nor is fear an explanation of what happened in the time of Hezekiah when that promise was fulfilled: 'Then Hezekiah and all the people rejoiced that God had prepared the people, since the events took place so suddenly' (2 Chronicles 29:36). If we accept that this promise and its fulfilment are evidences of the work of the Spirit, on what ground can we affirm that the Spirit was not equally at work before the time of the monarchy? The wholehearted response to the law given on Sinai, no less than the new life during the reign of Hezekiah, reveals a spiritual revival. Certainly, it is not to be compared with Pentecost in its impact and extent — see chapter 1 — but it is the same in essence: namely, a sovereign and unusual work of God's Spirit in the lives of his people.

Sadly, of course, that generation in the wilderness did not fulfil their great expectations. They had tremendous opportunities, but because of their disobedience they all died in the desert under the judgement of God. Revival can be 'felt and kilt' in less than a generation. It was their children who entered the promised land. Sadly also, that is too true of almost all revivals in the history of the church. Few outlive one generation and in this, Israel is not exceptional.

The settlement in the promised land also began in what appears to have been a spiritual revival. The generation that had grown up in the wilderness pledged loyalty to Joshua and the word of the LORD (Joshua 1:16-18), and the preparation for the conquest bears the marks of a people who were serious with God. According to Nehemiah 8:17 the celebration of the Feast of Tabernacles at the return from exile, a thousand years after the Exodus, had never been celebrated with such joy and enthusiasm 'since the days of Joshua'. Therefore, if there is evidence of a true work of the Spirit under Nehemiah it must say the same for the time of Joshua.

However, throughout this period of conquest there was a slow running down of spiritual fervour that left a poor legacy for the generation that followed. The people continued in the momentum of revival, but with an ever-evaporating zeal. The evidence of this is found in the second chapter of Judges. After the death of Joshua the people quickly became more and more entangled with the nations they had been ordered to destroy. The Angel of the LORD warned the people that their disobedience was bringing punishment upon them: 'When the Angel of the LORD spoke these words to all the children of Israel ... the people lifted up their voices and wept. Then they called the name of that place Bochim [meaning weeping]; and they sacrificed there to the LORD' (Judges 2:4-5). The weeping at Bochim was perhaps a reviving of the people at the close of the settlement of the land.

There are some ominous words in Judges 2:7: 'The people served the LORD all the days of Joshua, and all the days of the elders who outlived Joshua, who had seen all the great works of the LORD which he had done for Israel.' That prepares us for verses 10-12: 'When all that generation had been gathered to their fathers, another generation arose after them who did not know the LORD nor the work which he had done for Israel. Then the children of Israel did evil in the sight of the LORD, and served the Baals; and they forsook the LORD God of their fathers, who had brought them out of the land of Egypt ... and they provoked the LORD to anger.' The phrase, 'who did not know the LORD', does not mean that the people had no knowledge of this name, but that they had lost all understanding of its deep significance for Israel. Judgement and disgrace followed. Judges 2:15 tells us that 'they were greatly distressed'. So, throughout the Book of Judges we have a tragic cycle of events for nearly three hundred years: disobedience, disgrace, distress, repentance and deliverance. Thirteen times in the Book of Judges that cycle is repeated.

2 Chronicles 15:3-6 presents an alarming summary of those three hundred years: 'For a long time Israel was without the true God, without a priest to teach and without the law. But in their distress they turned to the LORD, the God of Israel, and sought him, and he was found by them. In those days it was not safe to travel about, for all the inhabitants of the lands were in great turmoil. One nation was being crushed by another and one city by another, because God was troubling them with every

kind of distress' (NIV). When the people cried to God, he came
to them in deliverance; that is not necessarily spiritual revival,
though occasionally it was, as we shall see. Judges 21:25 closes
with the words 'everyone did what was right in his own eyes.'
That was the Dark Age of Israel.

There is no clear evidence that any of the judges brought
spiritual revival to the nation, because the details of the people's
response are not given to us. Some judges were warlords who
gave Israel military victory over their oppressors, but others,
like Deborah and Jepthah, were clearly used to raise the level
of Israel's spiritual life. Deliverance and revival are not the same
thing; one is *for* the people, whilst the other is *within* the people.
The cry of repentance as Jepthah came to power certainly
reveals a true spiritual awakening. Together, all the people confessed their sin and threw themselves utterly on the mercy of
God: 'We have sinned! Do to us whatever seems best to you;
only deliver us this day, we pray' (Judges 10:15-16). Their active
response in destroying their idols and serving the LORD clearly
moved him to act for them.

It is too dismissive of the situation to assume that they merely
cried to God because of oppression by their enemies and that
there was little change of heart in them. God is not fooled by
pseudo repentance! In the light of the terrible spiritual, and therefore moral, conditions in the land, the fact that 'the Israelites
cried out to the LORD' can perhaps only be understood as a
spiritual revival.

We might suggest that many more periods of revival are
hidden in the Book of the Judges, and that without these the
nation would have sunk permanently into the degenerate paganism of the surrounding nations. The darkness of Judges was so
dark that almost any light could be seen as revival. Interest-
ingly, in spite of the cycle of gloom, the 'Angel of the LORD' is
referred to twenty-one times in Judges, which is more than in
any other Old Testament book. Where sin reigned in such

terrifying darkness, grace was always present. The only hope
was in the promise recorded in Judges 2:1: 'I will never break
my covenant with you.' That too may give us good reason to
believe that behind some of the judges lay times of true
awakening.

There are two more judges to mention. Eli judged during a
time of serious spiritual decline. This is nowhere more clearly
revealed than in the name of Eli's grandson who was born during
Israel's defeat by the Philistines when the ark of the covenant
of God was captured. The child was called *Ichabod* which means
'no glory' — because the glory had departed from Israel
(1 Samuel 4:22). Clearly by the time of Eli we are still in Israel's
Dark Age. It was generally a miserable time of unfaithfulness
among the priesthood and ignorance among the people. When
Samuel began his public ministry the nation had not seen spiritual revival for probably one hundred years or more — since
the days of Jepthah.

Samuel's powerful leadership was undoubtedly a time of
new spiritual life for Israel. As Samuel moved around his preaching circuit from Bethel to Gilgal, to Mizpah, to Ramah, we are
told that the LORD 'let none of his words fall to the ground'
(1 Samuel 3:19). That phrase means more than that his preaching was effective. It is equivalent to the not infrequent claim in
the Old Testament that all that the LORD has said will be fulfilled
(see, for example, Joshua 21:45 and 2 Kings 10:10). Samuel's
prophetic ministry was powerfully effective and revival began
with the people's sincere repentance: 'All the house of Israel
lamented after the LORD' (1 Samuel 7:2). The Old Testament
scholar S. R. Driver translated this verse 'All the people of Israel
went after him mourning or sighing.'[5] However, this had not
happened overnight. After the capture of the ark by the
Philistines and the destruction of Israel's military competence
(1 Samuel 7:2) at least twenty years had elapsed before the
people were stirred into spiritual activity.

That it was true spiritual revival is evident from Samuel's assessment: 'If you return to the LORD with all your hearts...' (7:3). It was a heart returning, supported by a significant change in their worship and behaviour: 'The children of Israel put away the Baals and Ashtoreths, and served the LORD only' (7:4). Here we have an Old Testament example of the effective ministry of God's Word leading to deep heartfelt repentance. Those two things, the power of God's Word and true repentance, are significant marks of spiritual revival.

The Kings of Judah

Saul squandered the spiritual gains of Samuel, and the first monarchy ended in unrelieved gloom. The Philistines commanded the land and what was almost the last act of the king was to dabble in witchcraft; as a result he and his sons lay stripped and mutilated on the battlefield. David brought new life and hope to the nation. His own personal spiritual life, despite his tragic sin over Bathsheba and Uriah, is revealed through the psalms attributed to him; but little is said of the spiritual state of the nation. Generally David led the people spiritually and positively, but there is no record of widespread national revival during his reign. The fact that there are psalms appealing for revival may imply that much of the spiritual health of the nation at this time depended on the forceful leadership of David himself.

How far the same is true of Solomon is a matter for debate. His personal piety, especially during his early years, is unquestionable; and during his wise rule the nation reached a high point of civilization and religion. However, evidence of widespread spiritual life among the people is lacking. The dedication of the temple gives a strong hint of a national stirring, and Solomon undoubtedly believed in God as a spiritually restoring God (1 Kings 8:33-53). It is probable, however, that since the general level of the nation's spiritual awareness was high during the rule of this spiritually wise king, there was little call for national revival. Revival is a sovereign work of God's Spirit after a period of spiritual lukewarmness. At the dedication of the temple an unusual spiritual zeal is evident by the extension to the time devoted to worship (1 Kings 8:65). This is matched only by the similar experience in the time of Hezekiah (2 Chronicles 30:23) which undoubtedly was a time of nationwide revival.

An indication of the high level of spiritual life among the people at the time of Solomon's dedication of the temple is seen also in 1 Kings 8:66: '[Solomon] sent the people away; and they blessed the king, and went to their tents joyful and glad of heart for all the good that the LORD had done for his servant David, and for Israel his people.' Again, this joyful response can be compared to 2 Chronicles 29:36 in the time of Hezekiah. If Psalm 72 is David's prayer for his successor, a prayer that God amply fulfilled, then the nation's spiritual life under Solomon was clearly at a high point.

At the division of the land during Rehoboam's reign in 931 B.C., Jeroboam established a monarchy over the northern kingdom of Israel. Among the twenty kings in the north, until Assyria finally defeated Samaria in 722 B.C., there was not one good king. Our attention should be directed towards the kingdom of Judah in the south because from there the line of the Messiah would come. The southern kingdom of Judah continued until the Babylonian captivity in 587 B.C. Here there were nineteen kings of Judah and they kept alive the dynasty of David. Among those kings in Judah were some outstandingly spiritual men: Asa, Jehoshaphat, Hezekiah and Josiah.

One objection that is sometimes levelled against the idea of spiritual revival during the monarchy is the fact that in those days of despotic, all-powerful rulers, a spiritual king did not necessarily require a spiritual people to achieve religious objectives. He could create changes simply by giving an order. This is true, but it does not follow that it was always the case. For this reason I prefer to speak of the changes under Josiah as reformation rather than revival, because the changes came from the top and there is little clear indication of spiritual life among the people. However, the spiritual events during the days of Asa, Jehoshaphat and particularly Hezekiah, reveal a very different story. Changes were not the result merely of a royal decree. We are specifically told that the people were in favour of reform with their heart and soul. The changes therefore were not simply for religious objectives, but were the result of a widespread spiritual transformation.

2 Chronicles 15:17 tells us that Asa's heart 'was fully committed to the LORD all his life' (NIV). But the fact that it became a people's movement is clear from 2 Chronicles 15:12, '[The people] entered into a covenant to seek the LORD, the God of their fathers, with all their heart and soul', and also from verse 15, 'All Judah rejoiced about the oath because they had sworn it wholeheartedly' (NIV). They sought God eagerly and they found him. Of the forty-one years of Asa's reign, revival continued for thirty-six of them. Revival, as we shall see again in chapter 3, is always a people's movement.

The same was true in Jehoshaphat's time: 'His heart took delight in the ways of the LORD' (2 Chronicles 17:6). This held true for twenty-five years during which time 'Jehoshaphat lived in Jerusalem, and he went out among the people from Beersheba [the southern border] to the hill country of Ephraim [the northern border] and turned them back to the LORD, the God of their fathers' (2 Chronicles 19:4, NIV) and 'The people of Judah came together to seek help from the LORD; indeed, they came from every town in Judah to seek him' (2 Chronicles 20:4, NIV). Here is a widespread, national response that can only be explained in terms of spiritual revival. 2 Chronicles 19:4

literally reads, 'he went out *again* among the people.' This must refer back to the officials who, in the third year of his reign taught 'the Book of the Law of the LORD' throughout Judah (2 Chronicles 17:7-9). The effect at that time was so powerful that even the surrounding nations feared, and the Philistines and Arabs — of all people — actually brought unsolicited gifts to Jerusalem (17:10-11). That, I believe, was a phenomenon without precedent in the Old Testament. This may well be a foretaste of Acts 2:5-12.

A similarly powerful work of God among his people occurred in the time of Hezekiah: '[Hezekiah] did what was right in the sight of the LORD, according to all that his father David had done' (2 Chronicles 29:2). The result of this spiritual leadership quickly spread throughout the nation, 'Hezekiah and all the people rejoiced that God had prepared the people, since the events took place so suddenly' (2 Chronicles 29:36), and 'The hand of God was on Judah to give them singleness of heart to obey the command of the king and the leaders, at the word of the LORD... The whole assembly agreed to keep the feast another seven days, and they kept it another seven days with gladness' (2 Chronicles 30:12,23).

During this spiritual experience in the time of Hezekiah we find all the marks of revival: urgency, preaching, conviction and repentance, prayer, worship, and evangelism. In fact each of these three occasions (Asa, Jehoshaphat, Hezekiah) lifted the people out of the previous years of spiritual and moral darkness. There can be no doubt that these three examples during the divided kingdom were powerful movements of God to revive the spiritual life of his people at a time when the knowledge of God had been almost eclipsed by the power of pagan religion. A king may reorganize religion without the support of the people, and consequently he may produce a reformation; that is certainly what Josiah accomplished, and to a more limited extent Joash also. But a king requires a spiritual people to make spiritual changes. A king can change the people's activity, but he cannot change their hearts. In the time of Asa, Jehoshaphat and Hezekiah, hearts were changed.

We cannot deny that these incidents were a clear work of the Holy Spirit in the life of the Old Testament community; but to deny them the descriptive noun 'revival' would seem to be pointless. As we saw in the previous chapter, there was undoubtedly more to come from Pentecost onwards, but these changes came about by a miracle of God's intervention by his Spirit.

Before we leave the period of the monarchy our attention must focus on the remarkable events in the city of Nineveh, the capital of the Assyrian empire. It is significant that Jonah was a prophet during the reigns of Jeroboam II in Israel and Amaziah in Judah. Jeroboam was an evil king (1 Kings 14:9) and Amaziah, who began well enough, soon 'turned away from following the LORD' (2 Chronicles 25:27). Consequently the spiritual life of the nation, both north and south, was at a low ebb. God sent Jonah away from Israel and Judah to a pagan nation. In one sense what happened in Nineveh was not revival in the usual sense of the word. It was not a reviving of the spiritual life of God's people, but it was certainly a great outpouring of the Holy Spirit to change the hearts of 120,000 people in a pagan city! God by-passed his own people and sent his Spirit to a godless nation to bring a whole generation to repentance. If this was a forerunner of what Paul referred to in Romans 11:11, 'To provoke [Israel] to jealousy, salvation has come to the Gentiles', then it certainly had that result in the life of Jonah! A similar call to national repentance is made by the prophet Joel (Joel 2:15-17), but Joel and Jonah were prophets of God; the command of the king of Nineveh came from a pagan king whose reign was steeped in the most cruel and debased idolatry.

By any standard, such an event today would be called revival. Some may prefer to call it a visitation, but the cause and effect is the same: a work of the Spirit for the conversion of what the nineteenth-century Scottish preacher Hugh Martin called 'the violent and bloody city' into a holy and God-fearing community. If we are to take the story of Jonah seriously, and Luke 11:32 compels us to, we must conclude that it is an account of a powerful work of the Holy Spirit, suddenly, in an unexpected place and with exceptional results.

After the Exile

In 587 B.C. Judah was taken into seventy years of Babylonian exile. The nation became a scattered, demoralized, and leaderless people. They were faced with a struggle for sheer spiritual survival. In Psalm 137 (NIV) we can hear how the nations mocked them:

> By the rivers of Babylon we sat and wept
> when we remembered Zion.
> There on the poplars
> we hung our harps,
> for there our captors asked us for songs,
> our tormentors demanded songs of joy;
> they said, 'Sing us one of the songs of Zion!'
> How can we sing the songs of the LORD
> while in a foreign land?

Rescue came as God said it would, through a royal decree of Cyrus, king of Persia. It was not only that God brought the people back from exile by a decree of a pagan king, but he turned the hearts of many of the people towards himself so that they wanted to come back. Psalm 126 reveals this: 'When the LORD brought back the captivity of Zion, we were like those who dream. Then our mouth was filled with laughter, and our tongue with singing.' Even though not all returned, in the light of the spiritual condition of the people who went into exile and the following decades of darkness and gloom which followed, that was revival.

This post-exile revival is described in the story of Ezra and Nehemiah. The walls of Jerusalem and the temple were rebuilt, but much more than this was accomplished. The events of those two books are mingled with waves of periodic revival as the various groups of exiles returned. When the zeal of the people cooled, the prophets Haggai and Zechariah, and later Malachi, were sent to rekindle their faith. What happened under the preaching of Haggai is recorded in Haggai 1:12-14: 'The LORD stirred up the spirit of [the governor of the city and the high priest and] all the remnant of the people.'

The joy and weeping recorded in Ezra 3:13 at the laying of the foundation of the temple created so much noise that it could be heard 'far away' (NIV), and at its dedication the note of joy was still present (6:16). Nearly twenty years later a second group of returning exiles arrived under Ezra the priest, and a new wave of revival broke out at a time when the people had begun to intermarry with the local inhabitants. The record of this is clear in chapter 10:1: 'While Ezra was praying, and while he was confessing, weeping, and bowing down before the house of God, a very large assembly of men, women and children gathered to him from Israel; for the people wept very bitterly.' This was followed by a thorough transformation in the heart and life of the people.

Nehemiah arrived in Jerusalem about the year 445 B.C., and a further wave of revival followed. This time Ezra read the law to the people from an open-air pulpit and the Levites followed it with a careful explanation of all that had been read (Nehemiah 8:1-8). The result was almost unprecedented! So broken were the people by the word of the law, that Nehemiah had to urge them to find their comfort and peace in the Lord

(v. 10) and the Levites had to 'calm' the people (v. 11). The early nineteenth-century revivals in Cornwall, England, reported the 'penitential pain' that a strong conviction of sin brought to the experience of many people; this not infrequently lasted for many hours until peace and joy replaced conviction and grief. This is precisely what we are reading here, almost half a millennium before Pentecost. When the grief of the returned exiles turned into joy, they celebrated the Feast of Tabernacles in a way that had not been known for a thousand years: 'The whole assembly of those who had returned from the captivity made booths and sat under the booths; for since the days of Joshua the son of Nun until that day the children of Israel had not done so. And there was very great gladness.' (Nehemiah 8:17). The same Holy Spirit who was at work in the time of Joshua was at work in the life of the nation in the time of Nehemiah. Later, at the dedication of the walls of Jerusalem, the extravagant joy of the people — men, women and children — could be heard 'afar off' (Nehemiah 12:43).

There can be little doubt that the period following the return from exile witnessed a significant spiritual revival among the Jews.

Isaiah 45:8 is not infrequently quoted as a description of revival: 'You heavens above, rain down righteousness; let the clouds shower it down. Let the earth open wide, let salvation spring up, let righteousness grow with it; I, the LORD, have created it' (NIV). At Albany, Georgia in 1831, William Sprague chose this as his text for the first of a series of lectures on the subject of revival.[6] He took this verse to refer primarily to 'a subject of far higher import [than the return from captivity], even the blessing of Christ's salvation.' But he had no need to go beyond the immediate application. Isaiah 45 is addressed to Cyrus, king of Medio-Persia, under whose command the Jews were given freedom to return and rebuild their city.

Conclusion

It should be evident from this brief survey that the story of God's dealings with his people throughout the two thousand years or more of their recorded history included regular periods of spiritual revival. It is perhaps no exaggeration to say that revival was the way by which God ensured the spiritual survival of his people. Their spiritual life at times was virtually eclipsed by the paganism around them and it was when God brought revival that he saved the people's faith from dying out altogether. Richard Lovelace is right when he claims that 'Under the old covenant the cyclical pattern of apostasy and spiritual renewal is one of the most obvious characteristics of the people of God.'[7]

We need to remember that the experiences of spiritual revival that we read about during the Old Testament era may not be all that God gave to his people. These are the only occasions for which we have sufficient records to be able to identify them for what they were. We are therefore not in the business of counting up the number of revivals God has given to his people during the Old Testament period. I am aware that writers on the subject of revival in the Old Testament differ in the list they would suggest; there is, however, close agreement in identifying those occasions of pre-Pentecost awakening. What we can say is that there are periods when revival was more or less a frequent experience (such as at the return from exile at the end of the Old Testament), and times when revival was largely absent from the nation's experience (for example, during the dark period of the judges). Some of the records are very scant and therefore, simply because we do not have sufficient evidence to identify it, we may not have classified as revival some periods that actually were revival.

To those who still deny the presence of revival in the Old Testament, we may well ask why remarkable events in the Acts of the Apostles are attributed to the work of the Holy Spirit, whilst similarly remarkable events in the Old Testament are refused the designation 'revival'? Would we enforce the same restriction on the word 'salvation' just because that doctrine does not reach its fullest revelation until the coming of Christ?

It is true that the examples I have given do not contain all the ingredients found in revivals during the story of the Christian church, although some of the descriptions used in the Old Testament narratives we have been considering are certainly not exceeded even in more recent revivals. But if there is a difference, it is chiefly one of potential. We cannot necessarily expect anything under the old covenant to be as rich and intense as under the new. We are living now in the age of the outpouring of the Holy Spirit, and nothing before Pentecost could be quite as expansive or glorious as afterwards. However, even if we do not expect to find in those Old Testament revivals the same extravagant outpouring of the Holy Spirit that we expect after Pentecost, the same ingredients will be more or less present. It could well be that if we had more detailed descriptions of the Old Testament spiritual revivals we would see just how close to modern revival they really were. In the previous chapter I suggested that Old Testament revivals may be thought of as 'pre-Pentecost pentecosts', in much the same way that we have pre-Incarnation appearances of Christ in the Old Testament.

In this chapter I have tried to establish that revival was certainly part of the life of God's people in the Old Testament, and not only an occasional or peripheral part. Revival flowed regularly into the story of God's people and was his chief means of ensuring their spiritual survival. Having identified some of the examples of this, we must turn now to the detail of this remarkable experience.

3.

The experience of revival in the Old Testament

In the first two chapters we established that it is correct to speak of 'revivals' in the period of the Old Testament. There are two reasons why we can do this. In the first place, whilst admitting that there are significant differences in the revelation of the work of the Spirit pre and post Pentecost, we must not fall into the trap of implying that he was needed any less for the work of regeneration and maintaining spiritual life. The dependence of God's people upon the Holy Spirit was the same under the old covenant as under the new; even though the people themselves may not have been aware of this. In the second place, there is undeniable evidence of his work in those high points of spirituality among the children of Israel, both individually and corporately. Unless we construct a completely new and opposite doctrine of human nature and of the work of the Holy Spirit for each of the Testaments, we must accept a significant degree of continuity. The discontinuity — the plus factor of Pentecost — we outlined in chapter 1.

The purpose of this chapter is to explore in more detail some of the identification tags of these Old Testament revivals; these are the hallmarks that reveal their true authorship. In other words we may ask, what are the common factors in these Old Testament revivals? There are at least nine in the examples noted in the previous chapter.

1. Revival follows a period of spiritual decline

Up to the time when 'men began to call on the name of the
LORD'(Genesis 4:26) there had been a steady decline from the
Fall. The universal Flood recorded in Genesis 6 - 8 reveals how
widespread the evil was even after the spiritual revival among a
part of the human race. Whatever significance we read from
Genesis 4:26, it is plain that there had been a long time when
people were not calling upon the name of the LORD. If suddenly, out of a dark period of spiritual and moral decay, men
begin to call upon the name of the true God in such a way that
God records it in his written revelation, then it is hard to know
how else we can describe it other than by the word 'revival'. It
may have been this revival in the time of Seth that held back
the anger of God and delayed the Flood. If men had not begun
to pray in the time of Seth, the Flood may have come much
earlier. Who can know? Noah was a direct descendant of that
godly line of Seth, and without the spiritual revival heralded in
Genesis 4:26 undoubtedly there would have been no one who
'found grace in the eyes of the LORD'.

At the time of the Exodus from Egypt, the spiritual condition
of the Hebrews would indicate that it was not only Pharaoh
who did not know about Joseph and the wonderful things that
God had done (Exodus 1:8). The Jews had all but forgotten
their patriarchal history and God's covenant with them. Even if
they were still using the name of the LORD in their worship, it is
clear that they could not appreciate its significance. This is the
best way to understand Exodus 6:3. It cannot mean that the
form of the word was entirely unknown to the Patriarchs, since
both Abraham and Sarah used it (e.g. Genesis 15:2; 16:2).
However, the Patriarchs understood God best under the term
El Shaddai, God Almighty (Genesis 17:1). What God was now
about to do was to invest the word 'LORD'with a deeper

significance than they had ever known before. Sinai was therefore a revival of what had been slowly suffocating during the
slavery in Egypt. The people's spiritual life was at a desperately
low ebb when they cried to God.

From the high point of Sinai there followed forty years of
decline that brought a new generation into the promised land.
The initial spiritual life of the generation of the conquest slowly
deteriorated, until the ominous comment in Judges 2:7 that
'The people served the LORD all the days of Joshua, and all the
days of the elders who outlived Joshua'— but not beyond!

The conquest of Canaan was followed by what we know as
the period of the judges. This was possibly the darkest time in
the history of Israel and the two brightest lights were Deborah
(Judges 4:1-4) and Jephthah (Judges 11:6), both of whom
followed periods of great spiritual apostasy. Similarly, Samuel
began to preach effectively at a time when the light had been
extinguished in Israel and this is witnessed by the daughter-in-
law of the old priest Eli who named her firstborn son *Ichabod*,
meaning 'no glory'. The loss of the ark of the covenant to the
Philistines was symbolic of the departure of the presence of
God.

In the previous chapter we noted that there is little evidence
of national revival during the reigns of Saul, David or Solomon. We may not be surprised at the first, but might have
expected a widespread spiritual revival under the leadership of
David and Solomon. On the other hand, the absence of any
account of a specific national revival during the reigns of David
and Solomon may prove the very point that we are making.
Two kings who were generally godly and wise set the spiritual
tone of the nation and there was therefore no need for revival.
Revival generally comes after a period of decline, not during
an era of strong spiritual life. Perhaps 1 Kings 8:66 provides us
with not just a reflection on the response of the people at the

dedication of the temple by Solomon, but with a cameo of their general spiritual well-being throughout the combined eighty years of David and Solomon's reign; it reads, 'They blessed the king, and went to their tents joyful and glad of heart for all the good that the LORD had done for his servant David, and for Israel his people.'

During almost three hundred and fifty years of the divided monarchy only three kings truly experienced revival: Asa, Jehoshaphat and Hezekiah. They each illustrate the fact of revival following a period of decline. Asa's father Abijah was a man who 'committed all the sins his father had done before him'(1 Kings 15:3). And sins they certainly were, including male cult prostitutes, and 'all the idols that his fathers had made' as well as the 'obscene image of Asherah' that his grandmother worshipped (1 Kings 15:12,13). Only a spiritual awakening could rescue the nation. Sadly, Asa's latter years were not so glorious as his former years, and when his son Jehoshaphat succeeded him, new light was needed in the land.

It was almost ninety years before Judah experienced another spiritual awakening following sixteen years of ungodly rule by Ahaz, the father of Hezekiah. Of Ahaz Scripture comments, 'He walked in the ways of the kings of Israel and also made cast idols for worshipping the Baals. He burned sacrifices in the Valley of Ben-Hinnom and sacrificed his sons in the fire, following the detestable ways of the nations that the LORD had driven out before the Israelites. He offered sacrifices and burned incense at the high places, on the hilltops and under every spreading tree'(2 Chronicles 28:2-4, NIV). Here is a picture of gross immorality and pagan darkness. Many of Hezekiah's own brothers had been burned in the fire of sacrifice to the god Ben-Hinnom. Out of this background came Hezekiah and revival.

When the northern kingdom of Israel was conquered by Assyria in 722 B.C. and Judah was defeated by Babylon in 587 B.C., the people were scattered across their known world.

Leaderless and dispirited, many of them began to absorb the pagan religions around them and they brought the local gods into their belief alongside the LORD. Young men like Daniel and his friends, who were determined to remain faithful to the God of Israel, could expect little by way of example from those who had been their mentors in Jerusalem (2 Chronicles 36:14). During that period of exile some remained faithful, but many scattered their religion on the ashes of the pagan funeral pyre. In 538 B.C. God changed the world government and Cyrus, king of the Medio-Persian Empire, allowed the Jews to return home. Out of the darkness of the exile, waves of revival are recorded in the books of Ezra and Nehemiah. The dark days of exile were over.

Whenever the people in the Old Testament experienced revival, it was because they had been walking in darkness for too long. Significantly, it was during the reign of Hezekiah's godless father, Ahaz, that the prophet Isaiah offered the nation its greatest hope with the promise that 'The people who walked in darkness have seen a great light; those who dwelt in the land of the shadow of death, upon them a light has shined'(Isaiah 9:2). Whilst undoubtedly pointing on to the coming of the one who was the light of the whole world (vv. 6-7), this promise nevertheless had a partial fulfilment during the reign of Ahaz's godly son Hezekiah. This is what we find throughout the story of the church right up to the present day.

2. Revival is accompanied by a desperate longing for God

We cannot be sure what '[calling] on the name of the LORD' means in Genesis 4:26, but given the spiritual and moral state that brought the Flood upon the world in Genesis 6 - 8, it is not hard to imagine the content of Seth's prayer. Similarly, the groaning and crying out for help by the Israelites in their Egyptian slavery (Exodus 2:23) was an urgent appeal which God answered with a spiritual revival that brought the Hebrews into a national identity that has continued to the present time. Sinai was the beginning of national Israel, which means that Israel as a nation was conceived in the womb of spiritual revival.

Prior to the call of Jephthah to be the ninth judge in Israel, the Spirit of God was stirring the people in an agony of repentance: 'Then the Israelites cried out to the LORD, "We have sinned against you, forsaking our God and serving the Baals"... The Israelites said to the LORD, "We have sinned. Do with us whatever you think best, but please rescue us now." Then they got rid of the foreign gods among them and served the LORD. And he could bear Israel's misery no longer'(Judges 10:10,15-16, NIV). That was an indispensable prerequisite for God to visit his people in the Old Testament with revival.

The same thing happened during the early ministry of Samuel. We are told that 'It was a long time, twenty years in all, that the ark remained at Kiriath Jearim, and all the people of Israel mourned and sought after the LORD '(1 Samuel 7:2, NIV). This was not twenty years of silence, because during that period Samuel was engaged in his regular preaching itinerary sowing the seed of God's Word. At the end of that time, the people were ready to mourn and cry to God; therefore Samuel said to the whole house of Israel, ' "If you return to the LORD with all your hearts, then put away the foreign gods and the Ashtoreths from among you, and prepare your hearts for the LORD, and serve him only; and he will deliver you from the hand of the Philistines." So the children of Israel put away the Baals and the Ashtoreths, and served the LORD only'(1 Samuel 7:3-4).

The same pattern can be found in the time of Asa, Jehoshaphat and Hezekiah. Asa 'commanded Judah to seek the LORD God of their fathers'(2 Chronicles 14:4). And 2 Chronicles 15:12 reports, 'They entered into a covenant to seek the LORD God of their fathers with all their heart and with all their soul.' Once he had confessed the sins of the nation, Hezekiah plainly stated his own commitment, 'Now it is in my heart to make a covenant with the LORD God of Israel, that his fierce wrath may turn away from us' (2 Chronicles 29:10).

One hundred and forty years after Hezekiah's prayer, Daniel, from his land of exile, was pleading with God for the nation. One of the greatest prayers in the Bible is recorded in Daniel 9. There is an urgency and a desperate longing in Daniel's inter-cession, which concludes:

> Now, our God, hear the prayers and petitions of your servant. For your sake, O Lord, look with favour on your desolate sanctuary. Give ear, O God, and hear; open your eyes and see the desolation of the city that bears your name. We do not make requests of you because we are righteous, but because of your great mercy. O Lord, listen! O Lord, forgive! O Lord, hear and act! For your sake, O my God, do not delay, because your city and your people bear your name (Daniel 9:17-19, NIV).

After such a prayer we are not surprised that revival was soon on its way, first during the time of Ezra and later through Nehemiah. Psalm 137 is yet another example of the kind of praying that led to the return from exile and the revival that followed. Accompanying revival or preceding it, there is always this heart cry and longing for God to act.

3. Revival begins with a leader

Invariably God uses leaders in times of revival. But the differ-ence between reformation and revival is that in reformation the leaders may impose changes, whereas in revival the leaders soon find themselves at the head of a popular movement. That is an important distinction to make. The mark of revival is a willing and enthusiastic response by the people. We may recall the leaders who were selected by God, for example: Seth, Moses, Deborah, Jephthah, Samuel, Asa, Jehoshaphat, Hezekiah, Ezra, Nehemiah, Daniel and Ezekiel. Some of the characteristics we discover in the lives of these great leaders are described very clearly in Hebrews 11.

They were all leaders of immense personal courage who were prepared to stand alone if necessary and do unpopular things until the people caught up with them. Moses stood alone on the side of God and sometimes he stood alone even against God: 'Yet now, if you will forgive their sin — but if not, I pray, blot me out of your book which you have written'(Exodus 32:32). Deborah, the prophetess of Judges, gave orders to a king. Samuel showed incredible courage over many years as a lone voice for holiness in a godless land. Asa even ousted his grandmother, the Queen Mother, because of her paganism. Jehoshaphat asked for God's advice instead of consulting the false prophets. Hezekiah changed years of ingrained practices that his father had built up. Daniel risked the wrath of five or six pagan despots, and the jaws of the lions, in order to take his stand for God. Nehemiah never flinched in the face of enemies who used swords, conspiracies and a fifth column in their attempt to topple him from power. He personally ejected Tobiah from the temple and warned what he would do with the Jewish and foreign traders if they opened shop again on the sabbath. Nehemiah was a man of uncompromising courage.

They were also men and women with a deep appreciation of the spiritual significance of history. That is an important point. These leaders often recited the history of the nation to spur the people on to action: Moses in Deuteronomy 29:2-18, Jephthah in Judges 11:14-27, Samuel in 1 Samuel 12:6-11, Hezekiah in 2 Chronicles 29:5-11, Daniel in Daniel 9:4-19 and Nehemiah in Nehemiah 9:1-38. The Old Testament leaders in revival rehearsed the stories of God's past faithfulness and the nation's disobedience. They had an appreciation of the importance and significance of their spiritual history. Those whom God has used in revival ever since, have been encouraged by the knowledge of what God has done in the story of his dealings with his people.

They were also leaders who were thoroughly committed to God's Word, to prayer and to personal integrity. The curriculum vitae of each of these men is in the Bible. Samuel speaks for them all, 'Here I am. Witness against me before the LORD and before his anointed. Whose ox have I taken, or whose donkey have I taken, or whom have I cheated? Whom have I oppressed, or from whose hand have I received any bribe with which to blind my eyes? I will restore it to you'(1 Samuel 12:3). Daniel stands as a man against whom even the revealing honesty of the Bible can find no fault and whose character was confirmed by a godless world: 'The governors and satraps sought to find some charge against Daniel concerning the kingdom; but they could find no charge or fault, because he was faithful; nor was there any error or fault found in him'(Daniel 6:4). None of the Bible leaders was without sin, but all of them were leaders of integrity whose lives were a model for the nation.

4. Revival always continues as a people's movement

In spite of all that we say about these great leaders, in each instance revival is a people's movement. That is seen by the response of the whole congregation. After the second giving of the law, Moses reminded the people of their response at Sinai which was 'We will listen and obey', and he reminded them also of the LORD's response, 'I have heard the voice of the words of this people which they have spoken to you. They are right in all that they have spoken. Oh, that they had such a heart in them that they would fear me and always keep all my commandments, that it might be well with them and with their children for ever!'(Deuteronomy 5:28-29). Whatever actions they may have taken subsequently, and God clearly hints at future failure, the whole congregation of Israel was serious in wanting to follow God. They had every intention of obedience.

After twenty years of faithful preaching Samuel saw that the people were ready to respond: 'So the children of Israel put away the Baals and the Ashtoreths, and served the Lord only'(1 Samuel 7:3-4). The same was true in the time of Asa: 'They entered into a covenant to seek the Lord God of their fathers with all their heart and with all their soul... [They] sought him with all their soul'(2 Chronicles 15:12,15). In the days of Jehoshaphat we read, 'From all the cities of Judah they came to seek the Lord'(2 Chronicles 20:4). In the time of Hezekiah, 'They sang praises with gladness, and they bowed their heads and worshipped'(2 Chronicles 29:30). In fact 'The whole assembly of Judah rejoiced'(v. 25).

After the return from exile, in the time of Ezra, 'A large crowd of Israelites — men, women and children — gathered round him. They too wept bitterly... The whole assembly responded with a loud voice, "You are right! We must do as you say"' (Ezra 10:1,12, NIV). We read exactly the same response from the people in Nehemiah 8:9-12. When Ezra read the law of God, 'Then Nehemiah the governor, Ezra the priest and scribe, and the Levites who were instructing the people said to them all, "This day is sacred to the Lord your God. Do not mourn or weep." For all the people had been weeping as they listened to the words of the law. Nehemiah said, "Go and enjoy choice food and sweet drinks, and send some to those who have nothing prepared. This day is sacred to our Lord. Do not grieve, for the joy of the Lord is your strength." The Levites calmed all the people, saying, "Be still, for this is a sacred day. Do not grieve." Then all the people went away to eat and drink, to send portions of food and to celebrate with great joy, because they now understood the words that had been made known to them'(NIV).

Events even approximating to this today would convince us that God has visited his people in revival.

The conclusion is that revival is not simply the result of changes imposed from the top. In fact, I would not attribute the word 'revival' to any response that appeared to be *only* obedience to the orders of a monarch or governor in the ancient world. I am aware of their autocratic authority. Revival is a wholehearted, enthusiastic response from the congregation, from a people longing to do what God says.

5. Revival is marked by a careful application of the Word of God

The elders of Israel responded to the voice of God from Sinai with a sincere determination to lead the people in whatever way God demanded; they pleaded with Moses, 'Go near and listen to all that the LORD our God says. Then tell us whatever the LORD our God tells you. We will listen and obey'(Deuteronomy 5:27, NIV). Even before this, the people's response had been the same, 'All the people answered together, "All that the LORD has spoken, we will do"' (Exodus 19:8). The next generation repeated almost exactly the same words to Joshua, 'All that you command us we will do'(Joshua 1:16-17).

During the dark period of the judges a knowledge of God's Word had not been lost entirely. To the king of Ammon, Jephthah retold the story of Israel at the Exodus and in his account, recorded in Judges 11:17 and 19, Jepthah quoted exactly the words of Numbers 20:17 and 21:22: 'Let us pass through your land.' According to 1 Samuel 3:19 - 4:1, Samuel relayed to the people all that God had revealed to him. Asa and the people determined to seek the LORD, 'and to observe the law and the commandment'(2 Chronicles 14:4). Jehoshaphat's heart was 'devoted to the ways of the LORD', and in the 'evangelism' that followed revival he sent his officials throughout Judah; they took 'the Book of the Law of the LORD with them [and] went throughout all the cities of Judah and taught the people'(2 Chronicles 17:9). The revival in Hezekiah's time was similarly based upon the word of the LORD, and it was noteworthy that the people had 'singleness of heart to obey the command of the king and the leaders, at the word of the LORD'(2 Chronicles 30:12). In addition, prophets were often among the people during these years of the monarchy, to give new revelation from God. He sent Azariah in the time of Asa, Jahaziel and Jehu in the reign of Jehoshaphat, and Micah and Isaiah during the revival under Hezekiah.

When the Israelites returned from exile in 536 B.C., they returned as a very different people. The nation had lost its city, homes and king. But the people had retained their book. According to Ezra 6:18 everything was done 'as it is written in the Book of Moses'. When they drifted spiritually or morally, the prophets Haggai and Zechariah, and finally Malachi, came to call them back to their biblical moorings. In Nehemiah we have the record of the people — 'men and women and all who could hear with understanding' — standing for half a day in the public square in Jerusalem whilst Ezra read from 'the Book of the Law'(Nehemiah 8:2-3). Then the Levites 'gave the sense, and helped them to understand the reading'(Nehemiah 8:8). The result was that 'all the people went away to eat and drink, to send portions of food and to celebrate with great joy, because they now understood the words that had been made known to them'(8:12, NIV).

6. Revival is accompanied by a conviction of sin and a longing for holiness

This is hardly surprising in the light of the centrality of the Word of God. When the people of God are confronted by his Word accompanied by his Spirit, there is always a longing to be obedient and a hatred of past failure. The elders of Israel insisted with Moses that if he would tell them all that God told him, 'We will hear and do it'(Deuteronomy 5:27). God clearly knew that this represented a genuine desire on their part because his response through Moses was in the form of a wistful desire that they might always think like this: 'Oh, that they had such a heart in them that they would fear me and always keep all my commandments, that it might be well with them and with their children for ever'(v. 29).

The Book of Leviticus presupposes a recognition of sin among the children of Israel. The various sacrifices promised reconciliation to their offended God on the condition that the sense of sin was genuinely felt and the repentance was sincerely meant. Prior to the leadership of Jephthah, Israel cried out to God, 'We have sinned against you, because we have both forsaken our God and served the Baals'(Judges 10:10). In fact their desperate case is revealed by their response when the LORD told them to cry to 'the gods which you have chosen'(v. 14). 'We have sinned,' they repeated. 'Do to us whatever seems best to you'(v. 15) — and they discarded all their false idols.

Hezekiah acknowledged the sins of his fathers as if they were his own (2 Chronicles 29:6-7), and his repentance is seen in the number of burnt offerings that he and the Levites offered following that prayer. In the land of exile Daniel cried, 'We have sinned. We have done wrong.' Ezra was found praying, confessing, weeping and throwing himself down before the house of God, and soon the men, women and children who had gathered 'wept very bitterly'(Ezra 10:1). Later, as the law was read and explained to the people, they wept continually and Nehemiah and the Levites had to calm the people saying, 'Do not sorrow, for the joy of the LORD is your strength... Be still, for the day is holy; do not be grieved'(Nehemiah 8:10-11). The Word had so broken them that there was a desperate conviction of sin and a longing to be in line with God. In the previous chapter we noted the reflection of this in the 'penitential pain' experienced by many when revival came to Cornwall at the beginning of the nineteenth century.

7. Revival transforms worship

Revival always introduced a new seriousness among the people — a sense of awe. At Sinai the people trembled because they feared God, and there is little reference to joy in their experience at this stage. In Deuteronomy 6, for example, the emphasis is upon obedience, fear and righteousness; almost every verse refers directly or indirectly to one of these. Love is given as a command in verse 5, but joy is not there. The word 'enjoy' at the end of verse 2 in the *New International Version* is not in the original. This is one of the experiences that increased as the spiritual life of the nation developed. However, there is an interesting retrospective comment in Nehemiah 8:17. The celebratory joy of the returning exiles is described as without precedent: 'Since the days of Joshua the son of Nun until that day the children of Israel had not done so [i.e. celebrated it like this]. And there was very great gladness.' This may simply refer to the fact that the people had not for a thousand years celebrated the Feast of Tabernacles by moving into their make-shift booths, but more likely it refers back to the joy expressed at the time of Joshua. Deborah's song of praise in Judges 5:11-12 mentions the singers at the watering places and the spontaneous songs that broke out after the defeat of Sisera.

One thing is certain: when the Spirit of God moved among his people, the first thing to change was their worship. It is likely that during the long years in Egypt true worship had all but ceased for most of the Israelites. Given the way many so quickly abandoned the worship of the LORD, or at least simply added him to the local deities during the period of the judges and during the exile after 586 B.C., it is hardly likely that pure worship fared any better during four centuries of Egyptian exile. The early chapters of Deuteronomy are primarily concerned to remind the people of the law, of their history and privileges, and to ensure that their worship remained pure. Commenting on the cruel and vile religious practices of the surrounding tribes, God warned 'You must not worship the LORD your God in their way... You are not to do as we do here today, everyone as he sees fit... be careful not to be ensnared by enquiring about their gods'(Deuteronomy 12:4,8,30, NIV). Moses had inherited a rag-tag group of runaway slaves. They had little true religion and therefore no true worship; they had no acknowledged leadership and no defined laws; they counted for nothing and were 'the fewest of all people'. Fifty years later he left them as a nation with organized leadership, clear laws for life, a firm understanding of the character of the true God, a knowledge of how to worship in fear and purity, and an eagerness to be obedient to the LORD. All this was achieved not merely by the rule of law and the charismatic leadership of Moses, but by the Spirit of God who, though infrequently mentioned in the records, was clearly at work among the people.

Whenever the nation experienced new life towards God, their worship changed. Asa 'removed the foreign altars and the high places, smashed the sacred stones and cut down the Asherah poles'(2 Chronicles 14:2-3, NIV). Jehoshaphat 'removed the high places and the Asherah poles from Judah'(2 Chronicles 17:6, NIV). In the very first month of his reign Hezekiah reopened the doors of the temple and re-established worship there (2 Chronicles 29:3,5).

By the time of the monarchy, joy had certainly entered into the worship of the people of Judah. Under Asa 'All Judah rejoiced at the oath, for they had sworn with all their heart and sought him with all their soul'(2 Chronicles 15:15). In the time of Hezekiah we read, 'Hezekiah and all the people rejoiced that God had prepared the people'(2 Chronicles 29:36) and the Levites 'sang praises with gladness'(v. 30). Later 'They celebrated joyfully... [and] the entire assembly of Judah rejoiced... There was great joy in Jerusalem'(2 Chronicles 30:23-26, NIV). It was described as exceeding anything that had happened since the time of Solomon (v. 26). This appears to have been upstaged in the time of Nehemiah when the weeping of the people was followed by such celebration and great joy (Nehemiah 8:12) such as had not been heard 'since the days of Joshua the son Nun'(v. 17) — one thousand years earlier! Ezra comments more simply, 'They kept the Feast... with joy; for the LORD made them joyful'(6:22).

8. Revival is always evident to the surrounding neighbourhood

Revival knows no hiding place and no disguise; the world knows what God is doing. This was the basis of Moses' plea to God in Exodus 33:16 (NIV): 'How will anyone know that you are pleased with me and with your people unless you go with us? What else will distinguish me and your people from all the other people on the face of the earth?' Moses knew that the spiritual health of the nation was vital for its testimony to the surrounding tribes. He knew also that God must be with his people if their spiritual life was to be right. When Moses prayed, 'If your Presence does not go with us, do not send us up from here'(v. 15, NIV), he was pleading for the presence of God to be revealed in a remarkable way.

When Asa assembled the tribes of Judah and Benjamin he discovered that 'They came over to him in great numbers from Israel when they saw that the LORD his God was with him'(2 Chronicles 15:9). He called together the tribes of Judah and Benjamin and when he counted them he discovered there were more than there should be; others had drifted down from Israel! This was incredible in the light of the fact that the north and south had been bitter enemies for generations. Even more unusual, during the reign of Jehoshaphat the surrounding nations brought gifts and tributes that the king, who had not defeated them militarily, had never demanded. The explanation is that 'The fear of the LORD fell on all the kingdoms of the lands that were around Judah, so that they did not make war against Jehoshaphat. Also some of the Philistines brought Jehoshaphat presents and silver as tribute, and the Arabians brought him flocks'(2 Chronicles 17:10-11). These were very unusual circumstances. In fact, the only other time such things occurred was during the reign of Solomon. On that occasion the nations were impressed by the king's renowned wisdom (1 Kings 4:34).

These were times of direct evangelism as well. Jehoshaphat went up and down the land from Beersheba to Ephraim and brought the people 'back to the LORD God of their fathers'(2 Chronicles 19:4). Similarly, Hezekiah sent out couriers throughout all Israel and Judah to invite the people to return to the LORD (2 Chronicles 30:1-10). Both the nations and the neighbours knew what was happening in Jerusalem. Revival cannot be hidden. This is always echoed in revival — for example, by the Waldensians in the Piedmont Valley in the thirteenth century, by John Wycliffe's 'poor preachers'in fourteenth-century England, and by the Moravian missionaries in the eighteenth century.

9. Revival rarely lasts beyond one generation

The generation that was revived at the Exodus died in the wilderness because of their subsequent disobedience, and a new generation had to seek God for itself. The generation under Joshua

remained faithful but, according to Judges 2:10, another generation grew up who 'did not know the LORD nor the work which
he had done for Israel'. These people ushered in the dark period
of the judges. Nothing followed the leadership of Deborah, or
Jephthah, except more darkness. The same generation that responded to the preaching of Samuel was soon demanding a
king and rejecting God as their leader. Hezekiah stands between a godless father, Ahaz, and an even more godless son
Manasseh.

Admittedly Jehoshaphat followed Asa but this is possibly
unique in Old Testament narrative, and there is a significant
note in 2 Chronicles 17:3 that the LORD was with Jehoshaphat
because 'in his early years he walked in the ways that his father
David had followed'(NIV). The tragedy of those three great
kings is that all three, Asa, Jehoshaphat and Hezekiah, were
less faithful towards the end of their lives; in the case of Asa,
this was after thirty-five years of revival. Revival can end by the
hand of those through whom it began. After the heady days of
Ezra and Nehemiah there followed four hundred years of
spiritual wilderness for Israel. It is instructive to study how revival ends and not just how it begins. God is as much sovereign
in the closing of revival as he is in the opening of it. After all, he
is the God of means as well as ends. He often allows the frailty
of men to destroy his work. The sinful failure of leaders can end
a revival, and sometimes revival is organized out of existence
by the church. At other times, however, God simply withdraws
his hand. Whatever the cause, each generation must seek God
for itself. He will not allow us to trade with the spiritual capital
of our fathers.

A rigorous critic may contend that all these hallmarks of Old
Testament spiritual awakening are merely a pale reflection of
Pentecost and of revival in the era of the church. I agree, but
my whole point is that they *are* a reflection. In other words,
whilst we would not expect to see in the Old Testament exactly

the same fullness of the outpouring of the Spirit, he is nevertheless there and involved in the life of the old covenant church.
Almost all the ingredients of Pentecost are here in the Old Testament. My argument is that as all Christian doctrines are introduced to us in the Old Testament, revival is no exception. The
light of revival may not shine so brightly as at Pentecost but the
light of revival was most certainly shining.

4.

The expectation of revival in the Old Testament

An historical view

So far I have tried to demonstrate that revival was an experience well known to the Old Testament believers, and that this was the way God ensured the spiritual survival of his chosen people. We have also seen some examples of Old Testament revival and some of the factors that were common to each of them. Whilst fully recognizing that there are still distinctives to be found in the New Testament era — a subject we dealt with in chapter 1 — my conclusion is that it is perfectly correct to refer to these occasions as revival. In the next two chapters we must turn to what is a difficult aspect and yet arguably the most important of all aspects of the Old Testament on this subject of revival, namely, did the Old Testament prophets, and therefore the people generally, expect revival? If so, did they expect it in their own time, or in a future time or at the end of time; and would this either precede or follow the return of the Messiah in glory?

This is an important question to answer because if the prophets expected revival only in the messianic gospel age — in the time of the church — then a number of issues follow. Firstly, this may be evidence that the prophets did not consider revival possible under the pre-messianic covenant; and secondly, if they did anticipate repeated periods of revival in the new covenant era then we can claim God's promises to this end. If in addition, or as an alternative, they expected a glorious end-of-time revival, then we can look forward confidently to the fulfilment of such promises at some time prior to the return of Christ. In other words, if the prophets spoke of an end-time revival, then we can be certain of the fact that one day, whether in our time or not, there will be a universal revival.

What makes our study of the expectation of the Old Testament difficult is that although many of the prophets speak of something that we must call a future revival of spiritual life, it is not easy to be sure exactly what they are referring to. To illustrate the point, here are two passages that are often used as the basis of prayer for revival.

> The poor and needy search for water,
> but there is none;
> their tongues are parched with thirst...
> But I the LORD will answer them;
> I, the God of Israel, will not forsake them.
> I will make rivers flow on barren heights,
> and springs within the valleys.
> I will turn the desert into pools of water,
> and the parched ground into springs.
> I will put in the desert
> the cedar and the acacia, the myrtle and the olive.
> I will set pines in the wasteland,
> the fir and the cypress together,
> so that people may see and know,
> may consider and understand,
> that the hand of the LORD has done this,
> that the Holy One of Israel has created it.
>
> Isaiah 41:17-20 (NIV)

Is this simply to be fulfilled literally, and if so, when? On the other hand, if we allow that the language is poetic, it appears to be a glorious promise of revival; but the question is: when will it be fulfilled? Isaiah 35 is similar, and generations of Christians have held out the promise, 'The burning sand will become a pool, the thirsty ground bubbling springs' (v. 7), when pleading for revival.

> I will heal their waywardness
> and love them freely,
> for my anger has turned away from them.
> I will be like the dew to Israel;
> he will blossom like a lily.
> Like a cedar of Lebanon
> he will send down his roots;
> his young shoots will grow.
> His splendour will be like an olive tree,
> his fragrance like a cedar of Lebanon.
> Men will dwell again in his shade.
> He will flourish like the corn.
> He will blossom like a vine,
> and his fame will be like the wine from Lebanon.
>
> Hosea 14:4-7 (NIV)

Clearly this is not intended to be taken literally; it claims to be poetic from beginning to end. But when is it going to be fulfilled?

At this point we must grapple with the complex subject of interpreting Old Testament prophecy. It is not sufficient to ransack the Old Testament in a hunt for any verse that appears to refer to revival, and then to hold it out as a promise that God is obliged to keep. We must keep stating that God is not obliged to keep a promise he has never made.

Understanding the millennium

It may not seem immediately appropriate, but we need to begin by understanding what is meant by the 'millennium'. The word is often tossed around in evangelical conversation without many having much understanding of its meaning. But we cannot go too far in discussing Old Testament prophecy without some understanding of this strange word. In biblical interpretation 'the millennium' refers to the period of one thousand years that is mentioned in the Book of Revelation chapter 20:3, 'He cast him [Satan] into the bottomless pit, and shut him up, and set a seal on him, so that he should deceive the nations no more till the thousand years were finished. But after these things he must be released for a little while...', and in verse 7, 'When the thousand years have expired, Satan will be released from his prison.' The problems begin as soon as we ask the questions: when will this be and what does it mean?[1]

What is known as the *premillennial* view states that Christ will come in glory and establish an earthly kingdom centred upon Jerusalem. For one thousand years he will reign as king and there will be a mass conversion of the Jews. Christ will therefore come *before* the millennium in order to establish his thousand years of earthly rule. That is why it is known as *premillennialism.* Closely allied with premillennialism, but clearly distinct from it, is a range of dispensational views that interpret all Old Testament prophecies concerning Israel in a fully literal sense and divides the whole of history into a number (from four to seven) of clear divisions (dispensations). The Jews themselves long believed that their Messiah would reign in earthly Jerusalem.

The *postmillennial* view believes that before Christ comes there will be a period (either a literal or symbolic one thousand years) of universal revival, a golden age of gospel success.

Because the belief is that Christ will come *after* the millennium, it is known as *post*millennialism. This golden age may come progressively as a slow build-up of gospel successes, or it may come as a sudden glorious revival. For some, it will be accompanied by a return to a system of government based on the Old Testament Law of God. This is the view of Christian Reconstruction. And for others, it will include the conversion of the Jewish nation through whom the world will be blessed.[2]

A third view, known as *amillennialism*, believes that the thousand years is a symbol of the period of the gospel age from Christ's ascension right up to the end of time — to the point where Christ comes in glory. The amillennialist does not disbelieve in a literal one thousand-year millennium but believes that we are in the millennium period now. Jay E. Adams calls it 'realized millennialism'[3], which is perhaps a better phrase to use.

Understanding prophecy

What you have just read is a simplistic way of explaining the millennial positions. There are many and wide variations of detail even among those who adopt a particular line of thought. But what has all this to do with the expectation of revival among the Old Testament prophets? Simply this: whenever we come to an Old Testament passage that appears to speak glowingly of revival we have at least six possible applications! There is a real danger that we should thumb through our Bible, find a wonderful Old Testament prophecy that refers to the desert streaming with water, blossoming with flowers and producing abundant crops, and conclude that it must refer to a promise of revival in our day. We then claim it as a promise from God. In doing so we have actually made a choice from six possible

applications without necessarily being aware of the basis for
our choice.
We will take *Isaiah 35* as an example.

The wilderness and the wasteland shall be glad for them,
And the desert shall rejoice and blossom as the rose;
It shall blossom abundantly and rejoice,
Even with joy and singing.
The glory of Lebanon shall be given to it,
The excellence of Carmel and Sharon.
They shall see the glory of the LORD,
The excellency of our God.

Strengthen the weak hands,
And make firm the feeble knees.
Say to those who are fearful-hearted,
'Be strong, do not fear!
Behold, your God will come with vengeance,
With the recompense of God;
He will come and save you.'

Then the eyes of the blind shall be opened,
And the ears of the deaf shall be unstopped.
Then the lame shall leap like a deer,
And the tongue of the dumb sing.
For waters shall burst forth in the wilderness,
And streams in the desert.
The parched ground shall become a pool,
And the thirsty land springs of water;
In the habitation of jackals, where each lay,
There shall be grass with reeds and rushes.

A highway shall be there, and a road,
And it shall be called the highway of holiness.
The unclean shall not pass over it,
But it shall be for others.
Whoever walks the road, although a fool,
Shall not go astray.
No lion shall be there,
Nor shall any ravenous beast go up on it;
It shall not be found there.
But the redeemed shall walk there,
And the ransomed of the LORD shall return,
And come to Zion with singing,
With everlasting joy on their heads.
They shall obtain joy and gladness,
And sorrow and sighing shall flee away.

Firstly, the prophet may be referring to something that will be fulfilled in his own day. Certainly he was preaching during, or close to, the time of Hezekiah as the following chapter makes clear. Hezekiah's reign saw a period of significant spiritual awakening.

Secondly, he may be referring to something that is going to be fulfilled later on in the Old Testament, beyond his own day. Many of the Old Testament prophecies are looking forward to the return of Israel from the Babylonian exile; that would be 150 years after Isaiah but still within the period of the Old Testament.

Thirdly, the prophet may be referring to the whole period of the gospel age of Christ and, under the picturesque language of Hebrew poetry, this may be his description of the benefits of the gospel. Jeremiah 31:31-34 would be another example of this — a beautiful description of the gospel age when God does not write the law on the tablets of stone as he did on Mount Sinai, but in the hearts and minds of men and women so that they want to please him. Though even this passage in Jeremiah is taken by some to refer to the privileges of God's final kingdom at the end of time!

Fourthly, Isaiah 35 may refer to the one thousand years during which Christ will reign as King in Jerusalem over a willingly submissive people. This is the premillennial position.

Fifthly, it may refer to the golden age of gospel success which we are not yet in but which will certainly come before Christ's return. This would be a postmillennial position.

Sixthly, your final choice is that the passage in Isaiah 35 may refer to heaven, the new Jerusalem. This is how some interpret Isaiah 11 and its reference to the wolf and the lamb, the leopard and the goat, the calf and the lion, with the little child leading them — it is picture language for the new relationships in heaven.

All this may be very confusing — even depressing — and therefore when we come to an Old Testament passage it is easy to conclude that with all these options it is, perhaps, not worth making the effort! On the other hand, if we think that it does not really matter, we should read through Isaiah 11 and 35 carefully and ask, 'What does it all refer to?' And when we have an answer to that question we should ask, 'Am I sure? How do I know?'

To compound our difficulty, commentators are far from agreed among themselves! E. J. Young suggests that the immediate fulfilment of Isaiah 35 is to be found at the return from exile (the second option above) whilst there is an ultimate fulfilment in the gospel age (the third option).[4] Calvin contemptuously dismisses the ancient view held by the Jews that their Messiah would reign in Jerusalem: 'I pass by the dreams of the Jews, who apply all passages of this kind to the temporal reign of the Messiah, which they have contrived by their own imagination.'

Whilst admitting that it may have a part fulfilment at the time of the return from exile in Babylon, Calvin has 'no hesitation' in concluding that it refers to the kingdom that Christ began here (the age of the gospel) and 'that which shall be completed at the last day'. He therefore combines options two, three and six.[5] The Hebrew scholar Delitzsch believes that in this chapter in Isaiah, 'The prophecy has now reached the highest point of its development.' Primarily it is intended for the exiles in their captivity, though he does not deny 'its spiritual New Testament thoughts'.[6] This would be option two.

In reality, of course, Isaiah 35 begins further back than verse 1! Significantly the opening verses of the previous chapter are picked up in Revelation 6:12-17; in fact these verses also clearly reflect back to Isaiah 2:19-21. The conclusion is not that Isaiah must therefore refer only to the end of time, as Revelation 6 probably does, but that the principles of judgement and restoration are appropriate whenever God delivers his people from oppression and subsequently restores them: whether this is after the exile or at the return of Christ, or at any time between!

A short history of postmillennialism

During the history of the Christian church those three main millennial views have been tossed backwards and forwards with the emphasis sometimes on one and then on another. Reformers like Luther and Calvin in the sixteenth century did not expect either a great conversion of the Jews or a golden age of success. Some of the Puritans in the seventeenth century shared this view, notably Richard Baxter of Kidderminster; but by then many of the Puritans believed in a postmillennial theology, expecting a time of universal revival just before the final return of Christ. They anticipated the conversion of the Jews, though not in a premillennial kingdom ruled by Christ on earth. On the contrary, they expected the steady progress of the gospel through periodic revivals to be so successful that countless millions of Jews and Gentiles all over the world would be brought to Christ. The whole earth would be full of the knowledge of the Lord as the waters cover the sea.[7]

An illustration of this postmillennial interpretation is found in *The Savoy Declaration* in 1658. This is a summary of the beliefs of the Independents, among them some of the best Puritans. In part *The Savoy Declaration* runs like this, 'We expect that in the later (sic) days, Antichrist being destroyed, the Jews called, and the adversaries of the Kingdom of his dear Son broken, the churches of Christ being inlarged (sic), and edified through a free and plentiful communication of light and grace, shall enjoy in this world a more quiet, peaceable and glorious condition than they have enjoyed.' Many Presbyterian Puritans, like Thomas Manton, David Dickson and Samuel Rutherford, identified themselves with that view. This postmillennial view was widely held by the eighteenth-century successors of the Puritans, including men like Jonathan Edwards, who expected the millennium to be a time of unprecedented revival. Edwards anticipated a time when 'There shall be universal peace and good understanding among the nations of the world... All the world shall be as one church, one orderly, regular, beautiful society.'[8] Such views continued to be held well into the nineteenth century by men like Robert Murray M'Cheyne in Scotland.

One example of the postmillennial position, which also shows the relevance that it has to our subject, is found in a series of lectures which were given in Glasgow in 1840 and which were published under the title *The Revival of Religion*.[9] The theme is best seen in the contribution of John G. Lorimer in Lecture 8 entitled 'Encouragements from the Promises and Prophecies of Scripture'. Lorimer was answering the question: 'How can we be encouraged to pray for revival?' His confident answer is that

Scripture prophecies encourage us to believe that revival is inevitable towards the end of time.

Lorimer asserts that the Word of God 'teems ... with assurances and prophecies of a day of coming universal religious revival'. He argues that this is what is meant by the promise to Abraham that 'all nations will blessed through your seed'. Similarly Moses, the Exodus, the Red Sea, Jordan and the Conquest are seen as impressive types and representations of the coming universal triumphs of the Christian church. Our attention is directed to Psalm 22:27 which in part reads, 'All the ends of the earth shall remember and turn unto the LORD: and all the kindreds of the nations shall worship before thee' (AV). Clearly that had not yet happened, not even in the nineteenth-century golden age of the British Empire on which the sun never set. Similarly Psalm 72:8 reads, 'He shall have dominion also from sea to sea, and from the river unto the ends of the earth' (AV). This has not yet been fulfilled. Isaiah 34 and 35 is seen therefore as a brief but most beautiful picture of the church under general revival.

Clearly then, what you believe about the time just pre or post the return of Christ does have an effect on what you believe about the Old Testament promises concerning revival. Lorimer is looking forward to 'a thousand years of joy' when Christianity is 'co-extensive with the population of the world' — a phrase that he does not attempt to explain further. However, Lorimer concludes that at the present rate of progress it will require a vast multitude of ages to accomplish this, so 'We are entitled to look for religious revivals in the future days of the church. They are essential to the fulfilment of prophecy. If there be no revivals the prophecy fails and with it the evidence of Christianity is compromised'.[10]

A similar optimism was found in America during the revivals of the early part of the nineteenth century. Two years before Lorimer delivered his lecture in Glasgow, Calvin Colton analysed revivals in America and wrote enthusiastically about the future. Condemning those who looked forward pessimistically, Colton encouraged his readers to expect the church 'to march directly to the conquest of the world' by a ' perpetual revival of religion — a revival without a consequent decline — an outpouring of the Spirit not to be withdrawn, or relaxed, so as to bring in all... of every community and every nation'.[11]

Edward Griffin, president of Williams College in New England, gave vent to his extravagant postmillennial hope in a sermon on Matthew 28:18-20 preached in September 1826. He looked forward to a time when 'Countless millions are shortly to awake from the sleep and darkness of a hundred ages to hail the day that will never go down. I see the darkness rolling upon itself and passing away from a thousand lands. I see a cloudless day following and laying itself over all the earth. I see the nations coming up from the neighbourhood of the brutes to the dignity of the sons of God — from the sty in which they had wallowed, to the purity of the divine image. I see the meekness of the gospel assuaging their ferocious passions, melting down a million contending units into one, silencing the clang of arms, and swelling into life a thousand budding charities which had died under the long winter. I hear the voice of their joy. It swells from the valleys and echoes from the hills. I already hear on the eastern breeze the songs of newborn nations... Come that blessed day. Let my eyes once behold the sight, and then give this worthless body to the worms'.[12] This same hope was embraced by Asahel Nettleton, who was greatly used by God in revival.

It is clear therefore how important revivals are to those holding a postmillennial position, and consequently how important it is that they can find the promise of revivals in the Old Testament. Before the church arrives at the great end-time revival, it will require a series of revivals en route. Lorimer is convinced that we must cry to God for revival, and all the promises of God about the big thing at the end imply that there have to be revivals along the way.

This is typical of the postmillennial view of the end of the age held by the Puritans in the seventeenth century and by their successors in the eighteenth and nineteenth centuries. Whether the millennium was literally a thousand years or whether that figure was symbolic of a fixed period of time known only to God, was uncertain.

A short history of premillennialism

During the nineteenth century a shift began to take place in favour of premillennialism. This shift can be illustrated by an event that happened in May 1828. Edward Irvine, a flamboyant and eloquent preacher, decided to give twelve early morning lectures, the subject of which was 'The Apocalypse'. It was an attempt to reassert premillennialism. The occasion Irvine chose was the General Assembly of the Church of Scotland in Edinburgh. He had no authority to give such lectures, and as he did not want to clash with any of the assembly meetings, he decided to hold his lectures at six o'clock in the morning. He obtained the use of a large church in the city and he packed it; he chose a bigger one and that also was filled. Even Dr Chalmers, with whom Irvine had previously worked as an assistant, was unable to get in. During those lectures Andrew and Horatius Bonar were converted to premillennialism.

Irvine's twelve flowery lectures to the crowded congregations at St Cuthbert's contained a spirited defence of premillennial hopes coupled with some strange uses of Old Testament prophecy. Daniel's fourth beast who was given the power to 'think to change times and laws' (Daniel 7:25, AV) was confidently reckoned as a prophecy of the British government's current attempt to repeal the Test Act! Few fully understood Irvine's theology, but it could be said of Irvine just as it was once said of the rhetoric of Queen Elizabeth I, 'Whilst no one could say exactly what she meant, everybody agreed it was worth listening to.'

Edward Irvine's personal story is a sad one. Sincere in his search for God, he became an extreme charismatic yet was never able to speak in the 'tongues' he so longed for, and many of his prophecies failed. Eventually Irvine lost all credibility and support.[13] However, he had presented the subject in a popular style and a drift towards premillennialism gathered momentum. During the nineteenth century, the published teaching of John Nelson Darby, the founder of the Plymouth Brethren movement, advanced the cause even more. Mixed in with all this resurgence of premillennialism was a heavy dose of 'dispensationalism' aided by the notes in the Schofield Bible. In this view all history can be divided into neat periods of prophetic fulfilment.

Premillennial views were especially popular among evangelical Christians during the last half of the nineteenth and the first half of the twentieth century. Sometimes extravagant interpretations of prophecy were retained and sometimes they were rejected; but for our subject the importance is that premillennialism did not need to lay such stress upon the necessity for revival, because the millennial kingdom of Christ will come when Christ returns as King. When he comes he will establish his kingdom so that he can personally superintend the affairs of his earthly rule. For premillennialism, revivals — desirable though they may be — form no *necessary* part of the eschatological hope and the end-of-time experience.

The significance of this is that during the period from the last half of the nineteenth century to the first half of the twentieth century the urgency of prayer for revival was to some extent lessened. There were some outstanding revivals during that period — in Wales in 1904 and East Anglia in 1921 — but the tendency was to refocus. We were not now expecting a marvellous golden age or a continual progress towards this glorious gospel success; on the contrary, the church looked for a time when Christ would come and establish a kingdom over which he would reign and from which he would superintend all the affairs of his kingdom on earth. To many therefore revival was less important than the hope of the millennial kingdom of Christ.

A short history of amillennialism

Partly as a reaction to some of the literalism of premillennialism in its interpretation of Old Testament prophecy and to some of the bizarre applications like those of Irvine and his followers, amillennialism received a growing interest during the middle of the twentieth century. When William Hendriksen first published his commentary on the Book of Revelation in 1939, it ran against the tide of popular evangelical opinion.[14] The 'Definite and sane principles of interpretation', which were claimed for Henriksen's book, became popular over the next few decades and amillennialism received strong support among younger evangelicals in the United Kingdom. However, it should be noted that premillennialism was still the main stream position in the United States — and still is. Under the amillennial view, many Old Testament prophecies were seen as referring to the age of the gospel rather than necessary promises of revival or of the millennium. At least it was a strong antidote to what Hendriksen called 'The many fantastic explanations that have cluttered around this scriptural gem (the Book of Revelation)'.[15]

The swing of the pendulum

A new movement swung the pendulum once more. The rise of the charismatic renewal movement from the late 1960s saw a slowly growing return to a postmillennial expectation. At first many of those who adopted charismatic renewal assumed that revival had come. Evidence of the 'gifts' was seen as evidence of revival. For this reason 'restoration' (of 'charismatic' gifts) and 'revival' became synonymous nouns. More recent years have cooled the enthusiasm of some who confused those two very different issues. Many charismatics who are driven by the existential philosophy of experience in preference to authority saw such phenomena as the 'Toronto enthusiasm' first of all as a 'rumour of revival' and then as revival itself. In reality it was neither.

Millennial history produces some strange bedfellows! The modern charismatic renewal movement is largely postmillennial not premillennial; on this issue at least, many charismatics hold a prophetic view not too dissimilar from that of the Puritans in the seventeenth century and of their successors in the eighteenth and nineteenth centuries. An example of this is found in a charismatic magazine. Four articles appeared under the title 'Global Revival', which is the kind of expression that the Puritans and men like Jonathan Edwards, Murray M'Cheyne and John Lorimer could have used. These articles gave a clear statement of a postmillennial hope. One writer closed with a reference to Zechariah 2:10-13 and with the words 'That is ultimate revival."[16] Elsewhere the same writer claimed that 'To release faith for revival I must find the basis for my prayer in the promises of God'.[17] Another writer added, 'It seems to me beyond question that the world is destined for a great and glorious revival in which multitudes will be swept into the Kingdom of God.'[18] He offered only Romans 11 and the final 'ingathering' of the Jews as any Scripture proof of that hope, but at least he himself was convinced 'beyond question'. This postmillennialism lies behind the upsurge of interest in revival among many charismatic Christians. Their interest is partly due to their prophetic hope that there is going to be a golden age of success and they see this as the fulfilment of Old Testament expectations.

A more recent view of a postmillennial revival was expressed by R. T. Kendall preaching in London in October 1992. He referred to 'the post-charismatic era' which would be a time 'when government and people in highest places will come on bended knee to God's people and ask for help... We are talking about something big... It will be a time when children will be sovereign vessels; an era when ordinary Christians will be equipped with prophetic gifts... We are talking about an awakening that reaches areas, people, places that heretofore were impenetrable without the aid of the media and public relations men, and the endorsement of high profile people.'[19] From a similar standpoint, in 1989 Wesley Richards records his conviction that 'The signs are clear: the countdown has begun to another great outpouring of the Holy Spirit. The best is yet to be.'[20] As early as 1983 Arthur Wallis, the grandfather of charismatic renewal, wrote an article in *Restoration* in which he claimed that the renewal movement was not revival but that a 'mighty harvest for the Kingdom of God' was yet to come that would put all else in the shade. His line of argument follows that of Lorimer, which is that without revival 'It is going to take thousands of years to see the kingdom triumph across the face of the earth.'

In more recent times Christian Reconstruction has provided a new perspective to the postmillennial picture. This view antici- pates a time when the whole world will be brought under the government of the law of God. One typical writer comments, 'The church triumphant from pole to pole, the government of the whole world by the law of God and then, after a long and glorious reign of peace, the Second Coming and the end of the world'.[21] Unlike most postmillennialists, the Reconstructionists have offered us literally millions of words on thousands of pages to explain just how the world will be governed during this postmillennial era. Their detailed analysis and application of Old Testament law is both exhaustive and exhausting.

From Jonathan Edwards to Wesley Richards and R. T. Kendall, postmillennialists have expected a millennial revival in their own day. If such a latter-day revival is really promised in Scripture, someone, somewhere, sometime, must be right. Meanwhile perhaps we should take a caution from the sad com- ment of J. F. Thornbury on that gloriously optimistic sermon by Edward Griffin in 1826, 'Griffin did not foresee that, within a few years, a poisonous rationalism would be imported from Germany and devastate all the great denominations. He did not take into account the seething cauldron of unrest which, within four decades, would burst forth into a bitter war, tear his country apart, and leave over six hundred thousand of its sons lying beneath the sod. Neither did he calculate that just around the corner were theological disputes which would fill the air and press, shatter the peace and unity of the Presbygationalist churches [meaning Presbyterians and Congregationalists], and have repercussions throughout the religious world.'[22]

However, a criticism of both pre and postmillennial views — not as a way of understanding Bible prophecy but as it affects revival and Old Testament expectations — is that if you view the millennium as a thousand years of gospel success just prior to the coming of Christ (postmillennial), or even if you view it as a time after the coming of Christ (premillennial), it actually does not help you to discover whether or not times of revival are God's plan for his church *throughout* history. The promise of ultimate end-time revival does not guarantee intermediate any-time revival. The assumption that in order to reach the goal of the whole earth being covered with the knowledge of God we must have regular revivals, does not offer proof that God has promised them.

In 1840 Lorimer asked the question, 'But how will the church arrive at this glorious millennium?', and he provides the answer, 'The Scripture seems to leave no room for doubt that there is to be the occasional outbreakings of sudden and singular revival.' But significantly he does not offer any scripture for it! He just makes the statement.[23] Again Lorimer says that we need such outpourings because each wave of revival will advance the church. In other words, each revival will build on the one before and take the church a step further towards this glorious golden age of success. But does history teach us that each revival builds on the advances of the previous one? The reign of Manasseh followed on from the revival under Hezekiah, and in half a century Manasseh undid all that was achieved during that revival and the nation was worse at the end of Manasseh's reign than it was at the beginning of Hezekiah's reign. When Josiah, Manasseh's son and Hezekiah's grandson, came to the throne the people did not even know where the law of God was — they had lost their Bible.

We learn the same from the history of the church. Where in the West of England today is the evidence of the 1814 revival in Cornwall — apart from scores of chapels that have been converted into private homes? Where is the residue of the 1904 revival in Wales today apart from fond memories and a national pride in religion? How widespread is the legacy of the revival in East Anglia and the eastern seaboard of Scotland of 1921? Even the fire of the 1949 and 50s revivals in the Western Isles of Scotland has sadly become a dying ember of diminishing heart religion. Of course, these are parochial examples, and it could be argued that the global picture is different. After all, the Great Awakening that may be said to have begun at Hernhut in 1727, led to a dramatic increase in world evangelization; and the Second Awakening that lasted for, broadly, one hundred years from the end of the eighteenth century, led to the great Victorian missionary movement. Nevertheless, I am not convinced that history supports the idea that God is building each wave of revival upon the previous one. Still less do we appear to be moving inexorably towards a glorious goal of universal gospel success. If that is where we must arrive, there is little evidence of it at present.

Lorimer believed that the promises of Joel, for example, go beyond Pentecost. In Acts 2 Peter says of the outpouring of the Holy Spirit at Pentecost, 'This is what was spoken by the prophet Joel.' Lorimer is convinced that 'Large as were the donations at Pentecost they can scarcely be said to come up to these promises. And hence we are committed still to look forward to effusions of the Spirit not less illustrious than those at Pentecost.'[24] But is that right? Does Joel 2 go beyond Pentecost? What does Joel 3:18 refer to, 'In that day the mountains will drip new wine, and the hills will flow with milk; all the ravines of Judah will run with water. A fountain will flow out of the LORD's house and will water the valley of acacias' (NIV)? That did not seem to happen in the time of the Acts of the Apostles. But will it ever happen? Or *did* it all happen at the time of Pentecost? Is it sufficient to say that Pentecost is a promised revival but of such a unique character that it is unrepeatable?

Lorimer concludes, 'We are entitled then to look for religious revivals in the future days of the church. They are essential to the fulfilment of prophecy. If there be no revivals the prophecy fails, and with its failure the evidence of Christianity is compromised.'[25] But is that a deduction not backed by scriptural authority? The only specific prophecies that we can claim from the Old Testament are those that refer to the return from exile and the outpouring at Pentecost and, assuming that we can accept the postmillennial hope, the one thousand years of Revelation 20. But none of these promises assure us of regular revivals throughout the life of the church. At the most we have prophecies of revival at the start of the church and the finish of the church; at Pentecost and in the glorious gospel age at the end; at its initiation and its consummation. Magnificent as these are we have to ask: is there nothing else to hope for?

We now need to ask ourselves, 'Does the Old Testament actually tell us that there are going to be revivals along the way?' In answering this question we may find a different and more satisfactory way of looking at the Old Testament prophecies and their bearing upon revival in the church.

5.

The expectation of the Old Testament — a study of the Scriptures

In the previous chapter we saw that our views of the end-time (eschatology) may precondition our interpretation of Old Testament prophecy. For those who believe that Christ will come and establish his personal and earthly rule in Jerusalem for one thousand years (premillennialism), it is tempting to read all Old Testament prophecies of revival as if they refer to this period. On the other hand, those who believe that before Christ returns there will be a golden age of gospel success (postmillennialism), the same passages may be seen as a promise of the revivals that must come in order to arrive at the final 'golden age'. Those who understand the one thousand years of Revelation 20:3 and 7 as a reference to the whole period of the age of the gospel (amillennialism) may assume that all Old Testament prophecies of revival refer to this period also. There is even an 'optimistic amillennialism' that confidently hopes for revival, and a 'pessimistic amillennialism' that believes the day of grace has passed! The importance of this for our subject is that our view of the millennium will significantly govern whether or not we expect regular revivals in the history of the church.

Postmillennialism hopes for and requires regular outpourings of the Holy Spirit in revival in order to press the church nearer to the day when 'the earth will be filled with the knowledge of God as the waters cover the sea.' Premillennialism and amillennialism are ambivalent about this requirement because their view of history, and particularly the end of history, does not demand either an ultimate big revival or many intermediate revivals to that end.

My task is not to resolve the millennial controversy but to show that there is another way of understanding the Old Testament expectations of revival. Many begin with the thousand years (the millennium) in Revelation 20, and first make up their mind what that is. Then they work back to the Old Testament and search for texts that look as though they might be referring to this particular idea of a millennium. Whilst it is generally a sound principle to interpret the Old Testament in the light of the New, the wide divergence of views in interpreting Revelation 20 may point to the fact that, in this case, we may be wiser to work the other way round. My method here is to start with the Old Testament and to show that throughout that period there was an expectation of periodic times of spiritual revival. In the light of my conclusion, our view of Revelation 20, whatever it may be, does not greatly affect our understanding of the expectation of revival taught both in the Old and New Testaments. We will discuss this under three headings: an expectation for *immediate* revival, an expectation for *intermediate* revival, and finally whether or not the Old Testament expected *ultimate* revival.

The Old Testament expectation of immediate revival

I am referring here to the confident hope of the Old Testament prophets that revival could or would come in their own day and at any time. The church in the Old Testament age, just like the church in the gospel age, went through barren periods when very few expected or were even interested in revival. I am not suggesting that revival was the constant personal expectation of the prophets, but the hope was always there in the Jewish Scriptures. God was a God of revival promises and that is the first point I would underline. The Jews learnt from their earliest history that God regularly revived his people.

My first evidence for this assertion may appear to come from an unusual source. In Genesis 2:3 God set his people a pattern by providing them with one day in the week when they should cease from labour. But this day was not just a regular day on which to stop work. When God gave his laws to the people he spelt out that one particular purpose of this day, though not the only one, was that it was a day on which everyone, including the slave and foreign resident, should be 'refreshed' (Exodus 23:12). The significance is that exactly the same word is used in Exodus 31:17 to describe God's action at the close of the six days of creating, 'He rested and was refreshed'. The form of the Hebrew word in both these verses is not common. It is found again only in 2 Samuel 16:14. David and his men were escaping from Absalom and they arrived at their destination thoroughly exhausted; there the king and his followers 'refreshed themselves'. The word is derived from the Hebrew for the soul or life of a man and it means to be refreshed or revived.

I am not suggesting for one moment that every sabbath was a time of spiritual revival in the fullest sense of the word, but I am claiming that within God's covenant plans for his people he deliberately worked in regular periods of physical and spiritual refreshment. At first this was a weekly sabbath, and subsequently there were extended sabbaths (Leviticus 25); it is these extended sabbaths that Paul refers to in Colossians 2:16. God's people knew that he was a reviving God; a God who, after their hard toil, would refresh them.

In the light of this it is no surprise therefore to hear Moses confidently talking of revival to the Israelites shortly before his death. He reminds the people of God's covenant of holiness, and he warns that disobedience brings severe judgement from God and disgrace in the eyes of the nations (Deuteronomy 29:24-28). In Deuteronomy 30:1-10 we have a description of what God will do when 'You return to the LORD your God and obey his voice ... you and your children, with all your heart and with all your soul.' God's response is not only one of restoration to their own land (vv. 3-5), but of giving them a new heart and soul: 'The LORD your God will circumcise your heart and the heart of your descendants, to love the LORD your God with all your heart and with all your soul, that you may live' (Deuteronomy 30:6). God offered his people a simple choice: at all times throughout their history they could choose death and destruction through disobedience, or life and prosperity through obedience. If they first made the wrong choice, at any time they could move from the bad to the good through spiritual revival which would be God's response to true repentance. God's way of bringing Israel from one state to the other would be by giving them new spiritual life. His promise in Deuteronomy 30:3 is best translated, 'I will put an end to your distress.' That promise was vital for the future life of Israel and it was never forgotten.

In Psalm 138:7 David reflects on Deuteronomy 30 by using a word that has as its root the same word Moses used when he encouraged the people to choose life. David said, 'Though I walk in the midst of trouble, you will revive me.' That is a good translation because the word used means 'to quicken' or 'give life'. David knew about the promise in Deuteronomy 30 and he used it in his time of need. The same word is used in Psalm 85:6: 'Will you not revive us again, that your people may rejoice in you?' Psalm 77 is a psalm that C. H. Spurgeon claimed was only for those experienced in the waters of affliction; in it Asaph based his hope for future rescue by God upon his know-

ledge of what God had done in the past, and his closing reference is to the leading of God in the time of Moses and Aaron.

This concept of revival is based upon the transition from the
bad to the good, from the barren to the spiritually fruitful, and
it was something that was well known in the Old Testament.
Jehoshaphat seems to have had this promise in mind when he
pleaded with God in the words recorded in 2 Chronicles 20:9,'If
disaster comes upon us ... we will cry out to you in our affliction, and you will hear and save.' Notice the certainty, 'we
will' and 'you will'. Such confidence can only stem from re-
liance upon a firm promise from God.

At the end of the history of Old Testament Ezra the priest
turned to the same word, 'revive' when he gave thanks to God
for the new spiritual life God had given to his people at the
return from exile: 'And now for a little while grace has been
shown from the LORD our God, to leave us a remnant to escape,
and to give us a peg [a fixed place?] in his holy place, that our
God may enlighten our eyes and give us a measure of *revival*
in our bondage. For we were slaves. Yet our God did not forsake us in our bondage; but he extended mercy to us in the
sight of the kings of Persia, to *revive* us, to repair the house of
our God, to rebuild its ruins, and to give us a wall in Judah and
Jerusalem' (Ezra 9:8-9). The same Hebrew word is used in each
instance where the word 'revive' occurs and the strength of this
word is seen by its use in 1 Kings 17:22 where the Lord restored to life the widow's son in response to Elijah's prayer.

In Psalm 80:3,7,19, the psalmist prays three times, 'Restore
us, O God.' Although a different word is used here it is one that
basically means 'to return'. Similarly in Psalm 85:4 the prayer is
'Restore us, O God of our salvation.' The whole of this psalm
clearly expresses a belief that there is a case to plead with God
and the psalmist expects a response. Restoration and revival

are synonymous terms here. Psalm 126 is a psalm of praise for the return from captivity and that great event is undoubtedly seen as a time of spiritual restoration and revival.

The same expectation is found in some of the public prayers of the kings in the Old Testament. This promise of Deuteronomy 30:2-6 is the basis of Solomon's prayer at the dedication of the temple recorded in 1 Kings 8:46-53. It was a prayer based firmly on what God had spoken 'by your servant Moses' (v. 53). Moses had been talking about times of backsliding and times of returning and revival; Solomon takes up the same theme and concludes with these words in 1 Kings 8:58, 'That he may incline our hearts to himself, to walk in all his ways, and to keep his commandments and his statutes and his judgements, which he commanded our fathers.' Compare this with 'The Lord your God will circumcise your heart and the heart of your descendants' (Deuteronomy 30:6) and 'You will again obey the voice of the LORD and do all his commandments' (v. 8). Solomon had already received the assurance of God that he would be faithful to the promise he had earlier given through Moses: 'If my people who are called by my name will humble themselves, and pray and seek my face, and turn from their wicked ways, then I will hear from heaven, and will forgive their sin and heal their land' (2 Chronicles 7:14).

Even when Isaiah is prophesying in the full hope of the Messianic age, he cannot stop himself from entering an urgent plea for immediate revival based upon the known character of God as the one who comes 'to the help of those who gladly do right' (Isaiah 64:5, NIV). That hope flows from his plea, 'Oh, that you would rend the heavens! That you would come down! That the mountains might shake at your presence — as fire burns brushwood, as fire causes water to boil — to make your name known to your adversaries, that the nations may tremble at your presence!' (Isaiah 64:1-2). The often quoted chapter of

Isaiah 35 must refer, at least in the first instance, to the revival that is recorded in 2 Chronicles 29 in the time of Hezekiah, king of Judah. This much is evident from the fact that the following chapter in Isaiah introduces the invasion of Sennacherib towards the end of Hezekiah's reign, which is recorded in 2 Chronicles 32. In reality it is doubtful whether Isaiah had any more understanding of the timescale than the people to whom he was preaching. The expected revival could have been at any time.

Alec Motyer is correct when he writes of Isaiah's prophecies, 'The whole book is a huge mosaic in which totally pre-exilic material is made to serve pre-exilic, exilic, post-exilic and eschatological purposes... [Isaiah] rarely offers dates because it is not useful or important that we should know the original setting of his oracles but only that we should discover how their inherent meaning subserves the unity of his message.'[1] Motyer warns us against the temptation of turning the deliberate mosaic into a text of perfect ordering and asks whether it would have been meaningful for the prophet to have said to his contemporaries, 'Be comforted, in two hundred years all will be well.'[2] He rightly reminds us that the two hundred years is our contribution to the discussion.

An even closer link with Deuteronomy 30 is found when Jeremiah wrote a letter to the Jews in exile, eight hundred years after Moses. His prophecy recorded in Jeremiah 29 contains the phrase, 'I will bring you back from your captivity' (v. 14). This is the same expression as that found in Deuteronomy 30:3. There is an intended link here, and Jeremiah doubtless had the promise of Moses in mind. King Jehoshaphat appears to have taken up the same promise when he affirms, 'If disaster comes upon us ... we will cry out to you in our affliction, and you will hear and save' (2 Chronicles 20:9). There is no uncertainty here because the king has just reminded God of his care over his

people in the time of Moses (v. 7) and this in turn reminds the
king of the promise given through that great leader. Jehoshaphat
was confident of restoration because of the promise.

Similarly, the prophet Joel appears to have Deuteronomy
30:2 in mind: 'When you and your children return to the LORD
your God and obey him with all your heart and with all your
soul...' (NIV). In Joel 2:12-17 the nation is encouraged to return
to the LORD on the basis of his known character of compassion
and mercy; they should 'gather the people, sanctify the congregation, assemble the elders, gather the children and nursing
babes...' and plead with the LORD to spare his people. There
are unmistakable reflections of Deuteronomy 30 here; this is
precisely what God had encouraged his people to do whenever they were in trouble. Joel 2:19, 23-24 is the exact fulfilment of God's promised blessing for a people who return to
him in repentance. The assurance of restoration from captivity
(Deuteronomy 30:4) is mirrored in Joel 2:18-27. Clearly this is
not a surprising response from the LORD but one that is to be
expected in the light of his known character (v. 13).

With the benefit of our knowledge of Acts 2:16-21 we may
understand the fuller significance of Joel's prophecy, but it is
not likely that the Old Testament prophet, reviewing the course
of Israel's history up to his day in the seventh century B.C.,
knew that the nation had more than half a millennium to wait
for this great revival. Without doubt the judgements of Joel
3:1-16 and 19-21 were expected in Joel's own day and the
material (or spiritual?) blessings colourfully described in vv. 17-18
would follow; therefore it is reasonable to assume that in the
prophet's mind the personal and national revival of 2:28-32
would also be immediate.

Daniel, in his prayer from the land of exile, went back in his
mind to the curses and blessings of Moses: 'As it is written in the
law of Moses, all this disaster has come upon us; yet we have

not made our prayer before the LORD our God, that we might turn from our iniquities and understand your truth' (Daniel 9:13). Then at the end of his prayer we have one of the strongest demands ever made upon God in the Old Testament record. Daniel had begun by saying that everything had happened to the nation as Moses said it would and then he concluded in this way:

> Now therefore, our God, hear the prayer of your serv-ant, and his supplications, for the Lord's sake cause your face to shine on your sanctuary, which is desolate. O my God, incline your ear and hear; open your eyes and see our desolations, and the city which is called by your name; for we do not present our supplications before you be-cause of our righteous deeds, but because of your great mercies. O Lord, hear! O Lord, forgive! O Lord, listen and act! Do not delay for your own sake, my God, for your city and your people are called by your name (Daniel 9:17-19).

Daniel looked for a reviving, and confidently expected it on the ground of God's covenant promises through Moses recorded in Deuteronomy 30. Similarly Ezekiel received the same hope which he confidently passed on to the nation: ' "I will put my Spirit in you, and you shall live, and I will place you in your own land. Then you shall know that I, the LORD, have spoken it and performed it," says the LORD' (Ezekiel 37:14).

This reference to Ezekiel is particularly significant. The prophet undoubtedly expected much more for the exiles than simply a return to the city of Jerusalem. In Ezekiel 37:14 he promised the exiles on behalf of God, ' "I will put my Spirit in you, and you shall live, and I will place you in your own land. Then you shall know that I, the LORD, have spoken it and performed it," says the LORD.' That this whole prophecy refers to the return from exile in the typically vivid language of the prophets (v. 12, for example), is undoubted. But it has a reference to much more than simply the nation returning to its homeland. The reference to the Spirit must refer to a spiritual revival, or else the language has little meaning at all. This is underlined by the extravagant promise of 39:29: ' "I will not hide my face from them any more; for I shall have poured out my Spirit on the house of Israel," says the Lord GOD.' We may rightly conclude that the ultimate fulfilment is at Pentecost, especially because of the similarity to Joel 2:28-29, but the whole context of the Ezekiel passage is the return from captivity. If the promise has no reference to that, it would amount almost to a prophetic deception. Our best understanding is to see the events recorded in Ezra and Nehemiah as a fulfilment of this promise, an example of Old Testament revival, and therefore what we have previously referred to as a pre-Pentecost pentecost.

One thing appears certain in all these examples: whether it was David, Solomon, Jehoshaphat, Isaiah, Daniel or Ezekiel, they all longed for and expected revival in their own time. They looked for immediate revival. They did not always get it, but they looked for it and expected it. The possibility of it was a living reality with them. They knew that if they repented and turned to God, at any time he might turn to them and revive them again because it was the nature of his promises and character to do so.

Too often we flatten this expectation by adding a timescale to the prophecies in the light of what we know with the benefit of the whole story of the Bible. We know — sometimes at least — when a particular prophecy was fulfilled, or when we expect them to be fulfilled. But the prophets and the people did not always have our advantage — though at times they did, as we shall see. In precisely the same way it is no criticism of Paul in the New Testament when he wrote as if the Second Coming of

Christ would be very soon. It was no business of his to know when, but only to ensure that the people lived in constant expectation of its any-time reality. After all, to adapt Motyer's wise words, it would hardly have been much comfort to the first-century Christians in persecution to hear, 'Be comforted, in something over two thousand years all will be well.'

The Old Testament expectation of intermediate revival

What I have already written may appear to preclude the next two sections. If the prophets did not know when their words would be fulfilled, how could they expect intermediate or ultimate revival? However, I suggest there were times when the prophet may have known, and at times certainly knew, that the fulfilment lay further in the future. Occasionally the prophets were given precise timescales in advance; Jeremiah 29:10-14 is one such example, and from reading this prophecy Daniel knew exactly when the exile would draw to a close (see Daniel 9:2).

Since the Old Testament is so full of prophecies we can only take a few examples, but I will try to take some significant ones. Isaiah 34 and 35 were prophecies given before the year 702 B.C. because that was the fourteenth year of Hezekiah's reign (chapter 36); almost certainly they should be located shortly after the defeat and exile of the northern kingdom of Israel in the year 722 B.C. Chapter 34 is a strong warning of God's final and terrible judgement on the nations, and it would have appeared ridiculously out of place at the time Isaiah gave it because the godless nations were having it all their own way and ten of the twelve tribes of Israel were already in exile and thoroughly disillusioned and defeated.

In chapter 35, which is entitled in the *New International Version* 'Joy of the Redeemed', we have an incredibly encouraging picture of God reviving and restoring his people. The question presents itself: when is this going to happen? Most Bible commentators seem to know the answer, although, as we have said, I am not at all sure that Isaiah did! The premillennial view suggests that this chapter is the picture of the one thousand years earthly rule of Christ. As we have seen, Calvin dismisses this as 'the dreams of the Jews who apply all passages of this kind to the temporal reign of the Messiah which they have contrived by their own imagination.' Calvin was unaware that many Gentiles would come up with a similar dream! The postmillennial view, represented by Lorimer, says it is a 'brief but most beautiful picture of the church under general revival'. The amillennialist will probably say that it is a picture, or symbol, referring to the age in which we are now living. Some, however, conclude that it is a picture of heaven.

Perhaps only one thing is beyond doubt: nothing like Isaiah 35 happened in the time of Isaiah, nor even during the reign of Hezekiah. Perhaps it has a partial fulfilment at the return from exile in 538 B.C. — one hundred and fifty years later. Isaiah was therefore looking at least for an intermediate fulfilment; he may not have expected it to happen in his own time, but it was coming and would appear not long after his death.

Two more passages in Isaiah clearly expect revival and it will be helpful to use them as examples of how we should apply Old Testament prophecy: not according to our preconceived plan, but according to the natural meaning of the passages themselves. The first is in chapter 41:17-20 (NIV):

The poor and needy search for water,
but there is none;
their tongues are parched with thirst.
But I the LORD will answer them;
I, the God of Israel, will not forsake them.
I will make rivers flow on barren heights,
and springs within the valleys.

I will turn the desert into pools of water,
and the parched ground into springs.
I will put in the desert
the cedar and the acacia, the myrtle and the olive.
I will set pines in the wasteland,
the fir and the cypress together,
so that people may see and know,
may consider and understand,
that the hand of the LORD has done this,
that the Holy One of Israel has created it.

The other passage in Isaiah is found in chapter 44:1-5 (NIV):

But now listen, O Jacob, my servant,
Israel, whom I have chosen.
This is what the LORD says —
he who made you, who formed you in the womb,
and who will help you:
Do not be afraid, O Jacob, my servant,
Jeshurun, whom I have chosen.
For I will pour water on the thirsty land,
and streams on the dry ground;
I will pour out my Spirit on your offspring,
and my blessing on your descendants.
They will spring up like grass in a meadow,
like poplar trees by flowing streams.
One will say, 'I belong to the LORD';
another will call himself by the name of Jacob;
still another will write on his hand, 'The LORD'S',
and will take the name Israel.

Virtually all Bible commentators, even those who divide the
Book of Isaiah into two at chapter 39, agree that chapters 40
onward stand together as one combined document. Isaiah 40

refers to the coming of the Messiah because it is the prophetic chapter pointing on to John the Baptist: 'A voice of one calling in the desert, prepare the way of the LORD, make straight in the wilderness a highway for our God' (v. 3). That much is clear. What is even more significant for our purpose is the fact that Cyrus, king of the Medio-Persian Empire is mentioned by name (44:28 and 45:1,13) as the destroyer of Babylon and rebuilder of Jerusalem. Since this is a despot who rose to power one hundred and fifty years beyond Isaiah the reference has provided a field day for the scepticism of Bible critics. However, it proves only that God can be specific when he wishes to be (compare 1 Kings 13:2). For our interest is the fact that the introduction of the name of a king not yet born, together with a prophecy for 'your offspring, and ... your descendants' (Isaiah 44:3, NIV) makes it certain that Isaiah knew that this promise was not likely to be fulfilled within his own lifetime. It would have to have what I call an 'intermediate fulfilment'.

The passages from Isaiah 41 and 44 (quoted above) that speak of revival, come between Isaiah 40 and 45. But what do chapters 40 and 45 refer to — the time of the Messiah or the time of Cyrus? There is very little doubt for us. So much of chapters 40 - 44 are actually used in the New Testament and applied to Christ (e.g. for Isaiah 40:3 see Matthew 3:3; for Isaiah 40:4 see Luke 3:5; for Isaiah 42:1-3 see Matthew 12:18-20; and for Isaiah 42:7 see Luke 1:79). The reference must be to the coming Messiah. Chapter 45 opens a new prophecy specifically relating to Cyrus. For Isaiah, then, both the time of the Messiah and the time of Cyrus are periods of glorious revival. He did not know when they would come, but that they *would* come was not in doubt. Isaiah is therefore looking forward to intermediate revival not ultimate revival; he was looking forward to revival both in the days of Cyrus, king of Persia and, though he probably was not aware of the full significance of his words, in the time of the Messiah also.

The prophet Amos provides us with a further example of this. Chapter 9:11-15 (NIV) is clearly about a time of spiritual revival:

'In that day I will restore
David's fallen tent.
I will repair its broken places,
restore its ruins,
and build it as it used to be,
so that they may possess the remnant of Edom
and all the nations that bear my
name,' declares the LORD, who will do these things.
'The days are coming,' declares the LORD,
'when the reaper will be overtaken by
the ploughman
and the planter by the one treading
grapes.
New wine will drip from the mountains
and flow from all the hills.
I will bring back my exiled people Israel;
they will rebuild the ruined cities and live in them.
They will plant vineyards and drink their wine;
they will make gardens and eat their fruit.
I will plant Israel in their own land,
never again to be uprooted
from the land I have given them,' says the LORD
your God.

When will this be? It may be at the return from exile under Cyrus, which was two hundred years ahead of Amos. Some claim that because the passage refers to rebuilding the city it is a picture of the earthly reign of Christ over Jerusalem. Others will suggest that it is a picture of the golden age of the gospel prior to the return of Christ. But we are not really left in any doubt what it refers to. At the Council of Jerusalem in Acts 15, James quoted from Amos 9:11-12 and concluded that its fulfilment had been when the gospel of Jesus Christ was preached among the Gentiles (Acts 15:12-18). The Scripture is its own interpreter here, and we must work from the Bible and not from our pre-planned scheme. James in effect says, 'This is that'; just as Peter on the day of Pentecost had said the same of Joel 2. Amos is therefore looking for intermediate revival beyond his own day but before the final end; though, again, the timing may have been beyond the knowledge of the prophet. It is in fact common among the prophets for them to give a prophecy that has an intermediate fulfilment (beyond their own time, yet before the Messiah comes) and a more distant fulfilment. Jeremiah gives us an example of precisely this when he is promising the return from exile and at one point 'overshoots' with the enigmatic reference to Rachel weeping in Ramah (Jeremiah 31:15; compare Matthew 2:8).

The Old Testament prophets believed therefore in a God of immediate any-time revival, and of intermediate future-time revival. Unknown to them the intermediate revival could be either at the return from exile in 537 B.C. or beyond this into the Messianic age — or both. But so far we have seen nothing of an ultimate, end-time revival.

The Old Testament expectation of ultimate revival

The question we are faced with now is this: will there be revival right at the very end, before the end of this age? Isaiah 34 and 35 provide us with typical examples of scriptures used by those looking for an end-time revival. Even if chapter 35 has a partial fulfilment in the time of Hezekiah or at the return from exile under Cyrus, the language may be far too rich and extravagant to be limited to those periods alone.

Calvin has no doubt as to its ultimate fulfilment when he comments on Isaiah 35, 'The Lord began some kind of restoration when he brought his people out of Babylon; but that was only a slight foretaste, and, therefore I have no hesitation in saying that this passage, as well as others of a similar kind, must refer to the kingdom of Christ; and in no other light could it be viewed, if we compare it to other prophecies. By "the kingdom of Christ" I mean not only that which is begun here, but that which shall be completed at the last day, which on that account is called the day of "renovation and restoration" (Acts 3:21).' When the apostle Peter says that 'There is a day of restoration and renovation coming' it is a very important point. Calvin continues, 'Because believers will never find perfect rest till that day arrives. And the reason why the prophets speak of the kingdom of Christ in such lofty terms is, that they look at that end when the true happiness of believers shall be most fully restored.' The way Calvin then proceeds to expound this chapter makes it clear that he sees it as a picture of the blessing of Christ through the gospel received now [3].

What Calvin means is that the revival referred to in Isaiah 35, whilst it may have an immediate fulfilment in the time of Hezekiah or an intermediate fulfilment in the time of Cyrus and the return from exile, it has a further intermediate fulfilment in the gospel age. But in dealing with Acts 3:20-21 Calvin is clear that these verses refer to something more, namely, the coming of Christ in judgement and the final restoration in heaven of all that God has promised through the prophets. For him therefore Isaiah 35 has an ultimate fulfilment in heaven.[4]

A more extended illustration of this is found in Isaiah 60 - 65. Isaiah 60 clearly refers to the gospel age and chapter 61 describes the work of Christ. It opens with the words, 'The Spirit of the Lord GOD is upon me, because the LORD has anointed me to preach good tidings to the poor; he has sent me to heal the brokenhearted, to proclaim liberty to the captives, and the opening of the prison to those who are bound.' We know that this refers to Christ's ministry on earth because at Nazareth our Lord himself read from this passage and announced, 'Today this scripture is fulfilled in your hearing' (Luke 4:16-21). Isaiah 61 must therefore ultimately refer to the ministry of Christ, and because the previous chapter stands inextricably with it, that too must refer to the gospel age. E. J. Young wisely comments upon chapter 60, 'The prophet is presenting the New Testament truth in figures belonging to the Old Testament. It would be incorrect, then, to interpret this verse as teaching a revival or reinstitution of animal sacrifice.'[5] We may add that it would be equally incorrect to interpret any of it in any other way than with reference to the benefits of the gospel.

Isaiah 62 therefore is not only a heart cry from the prophet, but it is a description of the purpose of the Messiah; it is Christ saying that he will not be quiet until the righteousness of God's people shines out like the dawn (v. 1). The theme of judgement and salvation follows through chapters 63, 64 and 65 with an intermediate cry for revival in chapter 64:1, 'Oh, that you would rend the heavens! That you would come down! That the mountains might shake at your presence ... [come down] to make your name known to your adversaries, that the nations may tremble at your presence!' At this point Isaiah brings us to a description of what he calls 'new heavens and a new earth' in chapter 65:17-25 which is linked with Revelation 21:1-2. It is quite clear therefore that when Isaiah arrives at chapter 65 he finds himself at the establishment of the Kingdom of God — a heavenly kingdom.

Here then is the pattern: Isaiah introduces the Messiah, quickly scans what we know as the age of the gospel, and then goes straight to the new heavens and the new earth. Jerusalem is not on earth — that is not even in Isaiah's mind — it is new heavens and a new earth that God will establish. Isaiah 66 is probably a final challenge to the Jews of Isaiah's day in the light of these great promises of the gospel and heaven. Nothing is hinted at in these chapters of a powerful end-time revival — glorious though such a thought would be.

Joel follows a similar pattern. We can have no doubt that some parts of Joel are fulfilled in the time of the New Testament. He was preaching possibly during the reign of King Joash (if so about 800 B.C.) and a summary of chapters 1 and 2 would be 'repent, repent, repent'. In chapter 2:19 the prophet introduces a time of spiritual revival. But the prophecy must be looking beyond the return from exile in 538 B.C.; in fact its reference must be beyond any reference to earthly Israel, because verse 19 has never been fulfilled from that day to this: 'I will no longer make you a reproach among the nations.' The next section, vv. 20-27, cannot refer to a millennium either pre or post the return of Christ, because verse 28 in the *New International Version* begins a new section with the words 'and afterwards' — and then follows the description of Pentecost. It is another picture of revival, and in Acts 2:17 Peter removes any doubt as to the application of this passage. We can only consistently read Joel 2:18-27 as another occasion where New Testament truths are presented in Old Testament language and the reference must be to the coming of the Messiah. If the alternative reading offered as a translation of verse 23 in the *New International Version* is correct, 'Be glad, O people of Zion, rejoice in the LORD your God, for he has given you a teacher for righteousness. He sends you abundant showers, both autumn and spring rains, as before', then we have a clear reference to Christ, and there is no possible reference to a millennial revival. Theodore Laetsch considers four possibilities for translating this phrase but prefers 'The Teacher unto Righteousness'[6]

Joel 2:28-32 is unquestionably a prophecy of the day of Pentecost. In vivid language (vv. 30-31) the unique events of that day are described. How far it can be taken as a description of the whole of the gospel age is a matter of debate, but one thing is certain: the obvious picture language of verses 30-31 should guard us against taking many of the symbols of prophetic language as having a literal fulfilment. Like a piece of music being transposed into a different key, Old Testament prophecy needs to be interpreted into a New Testament fulfilment. Isaiah 40:3-4 similarly provides an example of the extravagant picture language of the prophets for events fulfilled and recorded in the New Testament.

Joel 3:2 takes us right on to the Day of Judgement when he speaks of the Valley of Jehoshaphat. This valley is in the wilderness of Tekoa, south east of Jerusalem, where God destroyed Judah's enemies (2 Chronicles 20); the name means 'The LORD judges'. It was a symbol of God calling the nation to account. We should be aware of how much of Joel 3 is linked immediately with the Book of Revelation: Joel 3:13, 'Put in the sickle, for the harvest is ripe. Come, go down; for the winepress is full, the vats overflow — for their wickedness is great', is linked to Revelation 14:17-20, 'another angel came out of the temple which is in heaven, he also having a sharp sickle...' The winepress imagery is repeated here. Joel 3:16 is linked to Revelation 21:3. Joel 3:17 is linked to Revelation 21:27 and 22:3. Joel 3:18 is linked to Revelation 22:1-2.

So, Joel 3:18-21 is a glorious picture of revival, but since it follows the terrible Day of Judgement, it is the ultimate revival of the new Jerusalem when heaven becomes a reality for the people of God. It is like nothing on earth, it is heavenly Jerusalem. Once again spiritual blessings are clothed in Old Testament picture language.

Admittedly it is both easy and exciting to apply scores of Old Testament passages to an end-time millennium of gospel success. But is it accurate? Isaiah 2:2-4 (NIV) is yet another example:

In the last days
the mountain of the LORD's temple will be established
as chief among the mountains;
it will be raised above the hills,
and all nations will stream to it.
Many peoples will come and say,
'Come, let us go up to the mountain of the LORD,
to the house of the God of Jacob.
He will teach us his ways,
so that we may walk in his paths.'
The law will go out from Zion,
the word of the LORD from Jerusalem.
He will judge between the nations
and will settle disputes for many peoples.
They will beat their swords into ploughshares
and their spears into pruning hooks.
Nation will not take up sword against nation,
nor will they train for war any more.

It is Peter's use of Joel 2 that leaves little doubt as to the correct application of this passage in Isaiah 2. Joel 2:28 begins, 'And it shall come to pass afterward' which Peter chooses to render as 'in the last days' in Acts 2:17. But that phrase 'in the last days' contains exactly the words used in Isaiah 2:2. Since we know that Joel 2 refers to the gospel era, it is therefore clear that the description given of 'the last days' in Isaiah 2:3-4 is also a reference to the benefits of the gospel, and not to any final millennium. Confirmation of this is found in the similar, though not identical, expressions in 1 Corinthians 10:11, '[us] upon whom the ends of the ages have come', and Hebrews 9:26 (NIV) '[Christ] has appeared once for all at the end of the ages.' Both unquestionably refer to the age of the gospel.

Conclusion

The possibility of immediate any-time revival was always in front of the nation of Israel because of God's promises through Moses recorded particularly in Deuteronomy 30. True repentance could usher in a spiritual revival in the life of the people of God. Many of the prophets also looked confidently to the time of intermediate revival; either this would be at the return from exile, or well beyond their own day. Some looked on to the restoring of the fortunes of Israel during the days of the Messiah and the following gospel age, and they could only describe it in their extravagantly pictorial Old Testament language.

At that point they generally stop. They go no further than to begin with Jesus, the Messiah, and give an overview of the gospel age. Sometimes they may be specific, like Joel referring to the day of Pentecost. When they do look beyond the gospel age, the only thing they see is judgement, judgement, judgement and then heaven, heaven, heaven.

They have nothing else in mind. They do not give even a hint of ultimate revival apart from the final establishing of God's heavenly kingdom — that is the great thing they look forward to. The prophets offer the Messiah, the gospel age, ultimate judgement and the end. I find no indication of a golden age of spiritual revival and gospel success at the end of this age just before, or just after, the return of Jesus Christ. No millennial hope beyond the glorious age of the Messiah — the age of the gospel. Millennial views are impossible to substantiate clearly from Scripture and therefore they are uncertain to say the least. The widely differing views among biblical Christians may be evidence of this claim! However, the character of God and the strength of his promises, consistently understood, is where we should establish the ground for our hope.

In fact, I very much doubt whether the prophets worked to the same timescale that we can enjoy in retrospect. Ron Davies concludes, 'Revival, in the sense of the outpouring of the Spirit in a general way, does not appear to be an expectation for the Old Testament period itself.'[7] This assumes that Isaiah was well aware that he was *not* prophesying for his own time, or for any time prior to the coming of the Messiah. I am not so sure about this. His expectation may well have been immediate or inter- mediate. The concepts of Old Testament and New Testament, before and after Christ, are concepts that are peculiar to the Christian era. For the saints who lived before the birth of Christ, history was certainly pointing to the coming Messiah, but I doubt whether they had such a neat categorizing in their minds. In which case, who can know whether or not Isaiah hoped that he would live to see the fulfilment of his prophecy in 44:1-5?

The prophets certainly expected that, given the true repent- ance of the nation, God could bring revival at any time; this was always their hope. As we have seen, there is evidence also that they expected intermediate revival beyond their own time and into the gospel age. But they did not make this claim dir- ectly, because that was not their brief; their task was to prepare the way for the Messiah and to describe him and his ministry up to the final Judgement. Because God revealed himself to his prophets in the Old Testament as an any-time reviving God, there is no reason why we should not follow that principle through into the gospel age. If he was a reviving God in the Old Testament, why should he not be the same in the New Testa- ment? Everything God did by his Spirit under the old covenant he does more lavishly by his Spirit under the new. It is consistent with our view of the unchanging character of God that unless he reveals to the contrary, we may assume that the way he acted for his people Israel under the first covenant is the same as his care for his church under the second. It would be remarkably strange that the God who pledged himself to restore the spiritual condition of Israel when they called out of desperation for help, does not offer at least the same hope to the church.

Even if there is no specific golden age of revival on earth prophesied, the experience, examples and expectations of immediate and intermediate revival throughout the Old Testament give us authority to pray for revival at any time. In addition to this, if we find revival spoken of and expected in the New Testament, we can return to the Old Testament and use with even greater effect those passages that long for or promise revival, because our God is unchanging in his grace towards his repentant people. The character of God therefore is our ground for pleading with him to 'turn us again' and 'rend the heavens and come down'. It is our confidence for the bold cry, 'Awake, O LORD!' (Psalm 44:23).

6.

The New Testament expectation of revival

The New Testament covers just half a century of early church history compared with sixteen hundred years from Abraham to Malachi — and a lot more before Abraham; but the Triune God of the New Testament is the God of the Old Testament also. In Old Testament prophecy the coming of Christ and the birth of the Christian church is described as a period of great spiritual revival that was to be magnificently beyond anything known in the Old Testament. In our study we have seen how the prophets used extravagant language, often through the symbol of water, to describe revival. Some of the traditionally used texts for revival come in that form of imagery. One example is Isaiah 41:18: 'I will open rivers in desolate heights, and fountains in the midst of the valleys; I will make the wilderness a pool of water, and the dry land springs of water.' Another is Isaiah 44:3: 'I will pour water on him who is thirsty, and floods on the dry ground; I will pour my Spirit on your descendants, and my blessing on your offspring.' Those are two of a number of passages in the Old Testament where the possibility of intermediate revival is spoken of in the vivid imagery of God bringing springs of water on thirsty land.

Christ and his promise of revival

In New Testament terms these prophecies began to be fulfilled when Jesus stood up in the celebration of the great feast in Jerusalem and declared, 'If anyone thirsts, let him come to me and drink. He who believes in me, as the Scripture has said, out of his heart will flow rivers of living water' (John 7:37-38). The gospel writer, inspired by the same Holy Spirit, commented that by this Jesus meant the Spirit, 'whom those believing in him would receive; for the Holy Spirit was not yet given, because Jesus was not yet glorified' (John 7:39). It seems undeniable therefore that Isaiah 41:18 and 44:3 refer to revival, and that in John 7 Jesus took up the imagery and applied it to the giving of the Holy Spirit at Pentecost, the fruit of which runs forward into the history of the Christian church. In the same way that the prophets believed in intermediate revival as they looked on to Pentecost and the gospel age, so Jesus used that very picture in John 7. When he said, 'As the Scripture has said', he was clearly referring to those vivid pictures of God pouring water on dry ground. That could only have been fulfilled when Christ sent the Spirit to his people. This is the first evidence of the expectation of revival within the New Testament itself.

However, we need to ask a further question: did the expectation of revival end with the coming of Christ and the day of Pentecost, or was that a new beginning? Is there evidence from the New Testament that the prophets looked forward to more beyond Pentecost? And did the New Testament writers themselves expect something more? Part of our answer will be to fall back on the conclusion that we have already drawn, namely, that the Old Testament prophets saw God as a reviving God, and an any-time reviving God. Consequently, there is no reason why we should not follow that same God into the gospel age.

He has not changed his character. But that is an inference drawn from the unchangeable character of God. It is a very powerful inference — but is there nothing more that we can say?

Pentecost and the expectation of revival

In chapter 1 we saw that the promise of the new covenant heralded a new understanding, a new experience, a new commission and a new authority with the coming of the Holy Spirit at Pentecost. However, it is important to show that Pentecost was not an end but a beginning; in other words, what the Spirit did at Pentecost was not his final throw, but rather it was what be began to do. Just as the Gospels record all that Jesus 'began to do and teach' (Acts 1:1), so Pentecost heralded the continuation of that work by a new beginning.

There is one statement that I made in my book *Revival! — a people saturated with God* that I need to clarify; I wrote, 'The Acts of the Apostles opens with that unique flood of the Holy Spirit upon the church at Pentecost. This was not revival, it was bigger than revival'.[1] I suspect that that phrase 'this was not revival' taken out of the whole context was rather misleading. If the expectation of Joel 2:28-32 is for a great outpouring of the Holy Spirit, which it clearly was, and if its fulfilment was Acts 2, which it also clearly was, then Pentecost is *the* great revival anticipated by the Old Testament prophets, as we have already seen. However, the point I was trying to make was that Pentecost was a unique work of God that in many of its aspects could never be repeated. It was unquestionably a powerful outpouring of the Holy Spirit when one hundred and twenty disciples were saturated with God. I do not know of any revival where three thousand people were converted in one day under one sermon! Even the conversion of five hundred people after a single sermon by John Livingstone at Kirk of Shotts in 1630 cannot adequately be compared to Pentecost. At Pentecost, three thousand people from all over the Roman Empire, and beyond, came to Christ. This was God 'launching' his church. But the question is: was the Pentecost experience the beginning, or was it the end? Strictly speaking it cannot be repeated, any more than Calvary can be repeated, and our description of Acts 8 as the 'Samaritan pentecost' is therefore only loosely accurate.

On the other hand, I suggest that while Pentecost was a unique initiation of the new work of the Spirit, it was nevertheless a template by which revival can be measured. All the ingredients that we discovered in the Old Testament revivals were present on the day of Pentecost. It began with leaders who had a desperate longing for God and set themselves to pray (Acts 1:12-14; 2:1), and it ended as a people's movement (2:44-47). Pentecost was also marked by a diligent application of the Word of God, a deep conviction of sin and a desire for holiness. All this is plain from Acts 2:40-47. The work of the Spirit transformed worship and became evident to the surrounding neighbourhood. There was an awareness of God that filled everyone with awe. The new converts were also committed to the preaching of the Apostles, and the whole of the life of the early church was modelled by the Word of God. It is undeniable that Pentecost initiated the largest and fastest gospel migration in the long history of the church; evangelism was an inevitable result of disciple making.

Sadly, of course, like times of revival in the Old Testament, the immediate effect of Pentecost did not last beyond the first generation. We have seen this before. In fact it did not last too far into that first generation of Christians, and within twenty years there was already need for a fresh work of the Spirit among the churches. However, because that generation takes us virtually to the end of the New Testament, we would not expect to read much about revival before the close of the canon of Scripture. It is all the more significant therefore when we discover indications of promises and prayer for revival.

God has never allowed his people to live in permanent revival. There is perhaps a good reason for this. Revival is a time when God spoils his people by giving them all that they ask for and more. But God does not spoil his people for too long. The church would not be strong if it was always in revival. The disciples in that upper room were a desperately dispirited group and nothing less than revival could 'launch' the church for the fulfilment of the great commission. But the normal life of the church is tough. It was easy, even though costly, to evangelize after Pentecost when the whole atmosphere was charged with the presence of God, but it would not be like that for long. The normal days of the church are an excellent training time when God will see how easily we can be drawn aside to the counterfeit, the odd and the ridiculous.

However, because Pentecost was what the Holy Spirit *began* to do, it introduces us to a clear expectation of revival in the New Testament. In Acts 3:19-22 Peter was preaching in Jerusalem, perhaps only a few days after Pentecost. In the course of his sermon he made a highly significant promise:

> Repent therefore and be converted, that your sins may be blotted out, so that times of refreshing may come from the presence of the Lord, and that he may send Jesus Christ, who was preached to you before, whom heaven must receive until the times of restoration of all things, which God has spoken by the mouth of all his holy prophets since the world began. For Moses truly said to the fathers, 'The LORD your God will raise up for you a prophet like me from your brethren. Him you shall hear in all things, whatever he says to you.'

Peter's command was for repentance, and then followed a three-fold promise: forgiveness, 'times of refreshing', and the Second Coming of Christ. I believe that in these verses we can hear an echo of Deuteronomy 30:2-3: '[When] you return to the LORD your God and obey his voice, according to all that I command you today, you and your children, with all your heart and with all your soul, [then] the LORD your God will bring you back from captivity, and have compassion on you, and gather you again from all the nations where the LORD your God has scattered you.' Here is the echo in Acts 3:19, 'Repent therefore and be converted, that your sins may be blotted out, so that times of refreshing may come from the presence of the Lord.' In Acts 2:38-39 we have the same echo, 'Repent, and let every one of you be baptized in the name of Jesus Christ for the remission of sins; and you shall receive the gift of the Holy Spirit. For the promise is to you and to your children, and to all who are afar off, as many as the Lord our God will call.'

That phrase 'times of refreshing' in Acts 3:19 is highly significant. After repentance the promise is, forgiveness, times of refreshing and then Christ will be sent from heaven. The noun from which the word 'refreshing' comes means 'a breathing space or refreshment'; the verb can simply mean 'to recover one's breath, be refreshed or revived'. According to Strong's lexicon the noun means 'a recovery of breath, a revival'. The Greek lexicon of Walter Bauer similarly defines the noun as a 'breathing space, relaxation or relief'. It is therefore a word that has particular interest for us. In its context here, the word must primarily refer to spiritual renewal; after all, the true church of Christ will never enjoy its final rest in this world (Hebrews 4:1,9-10).

But there is more for us to consider here in Acts 3:19. The word for 'times' refers not to time in general (that would be the Greek word *chronos*) but to particular periods of time. In the first century there were two main uses of the word *chairos* which is used here. Frequently it was used to refer to a time of opportunity, but it could also refer to a specific period of time.[2] The two words are used together in Acts 1:7, where the first word 'times' is *chronos* and the second word, 'seasons' is *chairos*. Exactly the same expression and order is used by Paul (deliberately?) in 1 Thessalonians 5:1. The difference between the two words may be understood by comparing the expressions 'in our times' (a general use referring to an unspecified period) and 'at this time' (meaning 'now'). Here the word is plural, so the promise of this 'refreshing' is for an indefinite number of 'seasons'. The particular verbal form of the word translated by 'may come', is also interesting because it is exactly the same form as that translated in the next verse by 'He may send the Christ'.[3] The use of the word 'may' in modern translations is not intended to convey doubt and the *Authorized Version* in not incorrect by employing the word 'shall'. There is nothing doubtful about the fact of Christ's return, though for us the timing is uncertain. In the same way, times of revival are as certain as the return of Christ in that they will happen, but as uncertain as the return of Christ as to when they will happen. The verb in each case focuses on the event, or season, itself, without any hint as to how long it will continue or how often it will occur.

Peter is clearly looking beyond Pentecost, which was certainly the initiation of 'the promise of the Father' (Acts 1:4); but that was behind him at this moment in time and the apostle is now holding out a promise for the future. His promise is: forgiveness, seasons of revival, and finally the return of Christ. Peter is as certain that there will be times of revival in the history of the church as he is that Christ will come again from heaven. But he does not know when such times will be or how long they will last. That is exactly what we concluded about the Old Testament prophets; they believed in any-time revival but they did not know when, they did not know for how long, and they did not know how often.

An illustration of the unexpected nature of revival may be found in Acts 4:31. This was a new time of refreshing by the Holy Spirit for the disciples. The place where they were meeting was shaken 'and they were all filled with the Holy Spirit, and they spoke the word of God with boldness.' The question immediately is this: if they were 'filled with the Spirit' on this occasion, how could they be described just a few minutes before? I hardly think we can suggest that they were lukewarm and backsliding, but here is a new outpouring of the Spirit of God upon them that could only be described as a new infilling of the Holy Spirit. The place where they were was physically shaken and they spoke with a renewed boldness. That is a powerful description of what we would understand today as revival. What happened at Samaria in Acts 8 and in the house of Cornelius in Acts 10 may or may not be properly described as revival. Our decision on this will depend to a large extent upon whether or not we are prepared to accept that revival can sometimes begin among unbelievers. Certainly it did at Nineveh in the time of Jonah. If I am correct in concluding that the Ephesians described in Acts 19 were untaught Christians, then their experience can only be described as a spiritual revival.

From Peter's promise in Acts 3:19 I conclude that just as Old Testament revivals can be described as pre-Pentecost pentecosts (see chapter 5), so all outpourings of the Spirit in fulfilment of Peter's promise are post-Pentecost pentecosts. This is not meant to detract from the uniqueness of Pentecost, any more than the sacrifices of the old covenant and the application of the atonement of Christ to a sinner today detract from the uniqueness of Calvary. Pentecost, like Calvary, was a once-for-all occasion in history, the results of which are freely available today. Just as each converted sinner has his own 'Calvary encounter', so all who share in revival have their own 'personal pentecost experience'. The terms may be somewhat loose, but they are helpfully descriptive. However, the promise of Peter offers something bigger and more widespread than a personal pentecost. He expects times when the Spirit will come in the manner of Pentecost itself.

Paul's prayers for revival

Paul's prayers are remarkable. That he worried over the churches daily and prayed for them regularly he admits (2 Corinthians 11:28; Philippians 1:4), but unlike so much of our general or vague praying today, Paul was specific. He frequently told the churches exactly what he wanted for them, and his requests fitted precisely their needs. This last point is important. The requests Paul made were tailored to the situation that he knew to be current in each particular church; his prayers were not simply pulled off the shelf of pattern prayers. For this reason their content must tell us something about the needs of each church. But more than this, Paul's prayers were big prayers. The things he prayed for would transform the life of the church, and consequently they give us some idea of Paul's expectation of a new lease of life for the church, a renewal of spiritual vigour. We will consider just two of his prayers.

Ephesians 1:15-21; 3:14-21

Nowhere better does Paul reveal an expectation of new life for the church than in his letter to the church at Ephesus. In the first passage he prays for three things: a spirit of wisdom and revelation so that they might know God, an enlightened heart so that they might know the hope to which God had called them, and an enlightened heart so that they might know his incomparably great power.

It might seem strange that only ten years after the birth of the church in the most important city in the Roman province of Asia, Paul should think it necessary to pray that they might 'know God'. The word 'better', added by some translations is an intrusion into the text — that is not what Paul wrote. In 1526 William Tyndale well conveyed the meaning of this phrase by translating it, 'That God... might give you the Spirit of wisdom and open to you the knowledge of himself'. Already, in this affluent city with a thousand distractions, including a huge amphitheatre and the magnificent temple of Diana — the envy of the Roman world — Paul could see that their first love and enthusiasm were beginning to wane. An early echo of a later problem (Revelation 2:4).

So far this is a prayer that could be answered without the presence of what we understand as revival, but the reference to 'the working of his mighty power' ('his incomparably great power', NIV), prepares us for the even bigger prayer of chapter 3:

> I pray that out of his glorious riches he may strengthen you with power through his Spirit in your inner being, so that Christ may dwell in your hearts through faith. And I pray that you, being rooted and established in love, may have power, together with all the saints, to grasp how wide and long and high and deep is the love of Christ, and to know this love that surpasses knowledge — that you may be filled to the measure of all the fullness of God (NIV).

To know the width, length, height and depth of something provides us with all the dimensions we need to find out anything else that we may wish to know. And when we add to this the infilling — whether by that knowledge or by the Spirit, Paul does not say — 'to the measure of all the fullness of God', we have an expectation by Paul that is beyond our full comprehension.

It is for this very reason that the apostle continues with his doxology, 'Now to him who is able to do immeasurably more than all we ask or imagine, according to his power that is at work within us, to him be glory in the church and in Christ Jesus throughout all generations, for ever and ever! Amen' (NIV). The 'immeasurably more than all we ask or imagine' is clearly not a request for spiritual power for signs and wonders to startle the church and neighbourhood with unimaginable tricks of the supernatural. On the contrary, it is a prayer that the Ephesians might be so filled with the Spirit that they would experience 'the love of Christ' until they were 'filled with the fullness of God.' That last expression is almost inexplicable — which is presumably what Paul intended.

Unless Paul was praying for something that the Ephesians already had, which he clearly was not, then his hope for them was for an understanding and experience well beyond what they currently knew. If any church or churches today were recipients of the answer to this prayer they would undoubtedly be experiencing revival. The agency of this renewal of life is the Holy Spirit, 'the power that works in us'. This is a mind-blowing request by Paul. Notice how he begins with something that we can handle. Firstly, he wants us to be 'strengthened with might through his Spirit'; we can understand that and long for it. But Paul wants it to be a power that will enable us to grasp all there is concerning the love of God. But that is an overwhelming love, so Paul wants us to be saturated — inundated — with God. At this point the prayer is already beyond us. But just as our minds are struggling to grasp how big this might be, Paul adds that this is not all that he wants. He is also asking God to do 'immeasurably more than all we ask or imagine' (NIV). Yet he has not finished, because the apostle is asking God to do this 'according to [which means "in proportion to"] the power that works in us'.

I suggest that only in eternity will we begin to grasp the full import of a prayer like this. Meanwhile, is there a better description of what revival is than the answer to that prayer? Clearly the Ephesians were not experiencing all this, but equally clearly, they could. And Paul wanted them to. He was also convinced that it was within the sovereign hand of God to give, or else he would not have prayed such a prayer. This is surely Paul building upon the expectations of 'times of refreshing... from the Lord.' Like the prophets and Peter before him, Paul believed that there was always more that God could do for his people and that he was an any-time reviving God. In times of revival people are overwhelmed by the love of God, and it is commonly agreed that at such times the power of the Spirit is unexpected, unimaginable and inexpressible. That is precisely Paul's prayer.

Colossians 1:9-12

Paul had never been to Colosse and therefore we might expect his prayer for the church there to be very basic or at least general. In fact it is one of the most profound and compound prayers in the Bible. In the Greek there are nearly eighty words in verses 9-12 but only three sentences. In all, there are two main clauses each of which has two subordinate clauses, and each of these is further qualified; so there are eight separate statements in four verses! The grammatical construction of these verses is particularly complicated, and most commentators admit to being a little baffled by it! It is perhaps the best example of Paul's mind in overdrive.

In this prayer Paul was motivated by a good cause. The Christians at Colosse were known particularly for two things:

'faith in Christ Jesus and … love for all the saints' (v. 4). They had learned the gospel from Epaphras (v. 7), and the work was progressing most satisfactorily (v. 6). It was, in fact, the success of the gospel that was the cause of Paul's prayer (v. 9). In other words, he was anxious to build upon success. The significance of this is that Paul was not praying for an ailing church; the church at Colosse was vigorous, healthy and growing; the quality of its life was renowned. If this reveals anything at all, it demonstrates that Paul was never a man to be complacent; where there was life he wanted more life, and where there was growth he wanted more growth. It may also remind us that not only the church in decline can pray for revival.

Paul's two main prayers for this church, which he had only heard about, were that they would be 'filled with the knowledge of [God's] will' (v. 9) and 'strengthened with all might' (v. 11). But, as with the church at Ephesus, the knowledge and power were not for personal entertainment. Paul wanted them to experience 'wisdom and spiritual understanding' and 'might, according to [God's] glorious power', so that they would live lives that were 'worthy of the Lord' (the word *axios* means of equivalent weight or equal value) and fully pleasing to the Lord. Paul describes this as 'being fruitful in every good work' and 'increasing in the knowledge of God' (v. 10). The key to all of this is that the church might be 'strengthened with all might, according to his glorious power' (v. 11). What Paul actually says here is, 'empowered with all power according to the dominion of his glory'; here the word for 'power' (*dunamis*), which is repeated, refers to the inherent power of God, and the word for 'might' (*kratos*) refers to his manifested power. In the first century this word was often used with reference to the gods or emperors,[4] and both Paul and Peter (1 Peter 4:11 'dominion') unashamedly turn it to Christian use. The inherent power of God is seen (manifested) in the creation and the resurrection, in both of which the Holy Spirit was an active agent (Genesis 1:2 and 1 Peter 3:18). However, Paul makes it clear that in the case of the Christians at Colosse he is praying that the inherent power of the Spirit would be manifested in their 'great endurance … patience and [joy]' (v. 11, NIV).

What has all this to do with revival? That this is a 'big' prayer is undeniable. How far the church at Colosse received the full benefit of God answering Paul's prayer on their behalf will never be known to us; the fact that Colosse is not one of the churches mentioned in the seven letters of the apostle John (Revelation 2 - 3) could imply their continued steady growth. However, whether or not God answered Paul's prayer, this was certainly the apostle's longing for them; and the result intended would have been a new breath of life to a young church. Unknown to Paul, within a few years of his letter the whole area around this city would be devastated by an earthquake, and their quality of endurance, patience and joy would be severely tested. Everyone would soon see whether these Christians pleased their Lord and bore fruit in every good work. Perhaps, unknowingly, Paul's prayer was a preparation for what was to follow; historically, revival often precedes a time of persecution or suffering.

What must be clear is that Paul knew the 'size' of his prayer and was aware that if God answered, it would transform the life of even this vigorous and healthy church. As part of our definition of revival, we often assume that it comes only to a church that is in a weak state of decline. This is generally true, and both the Bible and history have shown us that. However, it would be unwise to limit God to that model, and equally foolish for the healthy church to assume that it has all that it needs of God. There is surely a place in the life of every church to plead with God for more knowledge of himself and a greater experience of his Holy Spirit. And there is a good reason for this. How a church judges its spiritual condition is almost always relative to its contemporary scene. No doubt the church at Colosse could think of itself with satisfaction if it looked at the churches in Galatia or Corinth. But Paul knew better than that. He was aware that even the church at Colosse could go on to a deeper and higher quality of life and experience of God.

In a previous chapter we referred to Spurgeon's wise comment that, in a healthy church, 'Their piety ought to need no reviving.' The great Victorian preacher went on to urge that such a church 'should aspire to a higher blessing, a richer mercy, than a mere revival. They should be asking for growth in grace, for increase of strength, and for greater success.' Perhaps Paul would see little difference between this and revival itself. After all, 'a mere revival' will always be accompanied by growth in grace, increase in strength and greater success. However, Spurgeon, as usual, makes a good point, in that revival and maturity do not always go hand in hand; a revived church must long and pray for maturity — and this is precisely the point at which many revivals in history have ended in failure. I think Spurgeon would endorse my phrase, 'a satisfied dissatisfaction'. A contented dissatisfaction should be the hallmark of even the healthiest church. Mere contentment will lead to complacency — the very thing for which, years later, the church at Ephesus was accused (Revelation 2:1-7) and even more so the church at Laodicea (Revelation 3:14-22).

An invitation to the church prayer meetings to pray for revival is often a sure way to create silence! Evangelical churches today just do not know what to pray for under that heading. This is perfectly understandable if a church has never been told what revival is, biblically and historically. However, many of our prayer meetings would take on a new purpose and dynamic if attention were drawn to these paradigm prayers of Paul. If we spent a few minutes understanding what it was that Paul was expecting, and then prayed his prayers as our own, we may well receive answers that would be far more valuable than most of the things that are traditionally brought before

God at our weekly prayer meetings. If ever we do not know how to pray as we should, these model prayers in Ephesians 1 and 3, and Colossians 1 (and Philippians 1:9-11) would prove an excellent place to begin.

The need of the first-century church for revival

Before the close of the New Testament there were many churches across Asia that were certainly in desperate need of revival. From the second and third chapters of Revelation that much is clear. The warning of the Spirit to the outwardly healthy church at Ephesus is this, 'Nevertheless I have this against you, that you have left your first love. Remember therefore from where you have fallen; repent and do the first works, or else I will come to you quickly and remove your lampstand from its place — unless you repent' (Revelation 2:4-5). The Ephesian church enjoyed some of those very qualities that Paul included in his prayer for the church at Colosse: it was hard-working, enduring, patient and holy. It looked excellent. Yet in reality the church was cold and spiritually dry. A church like this surely needs fresh life and vitality — a season of refreshing. And this new life would begin with repentance. God's offer was that if they turned to him, there would be something far better for them.

The Spirit gave a similar warning to the church at Pergamum. Their loyalty under persecution in the past (Revelation 2:13) could not disguise the fact that they had allowed the Nicolaitans to settle in the church and spread the devastating doctrine of compromise with pagan religion and morality. This could be compared only to the false prophet Balaam in the Old Testament (vv. 14-15). Their journey into the blessing of God must also begin with repentance (v. 16).

The church at Sardis was ordered to 'be watchful, and strengthen the things which remain, that are ready to die' (3:2).

Its condition was perilous, having a reputation for spiritual life but in reality being spiritually as good as dead. God saw through their veneer and urged them to come alive to the reality of their situation before it was too late. Here was a church in urgent need of a time of refreshing, and the offer was there for them to 'remember ... and repent' (3:3).

However, there were two churches that were given no command to repent with the offer of new life in return. The church at Smyrna (2:8-11) was the only church among the seven that was offered no respite from the relentless persecution which they had been facing so bravely. Thyatira, on the other hand, appears to have been hi-jacked by the spiritual descendants of Jezebel and there remained only judgement for these people and an encouragement for the faithful to 'hold fast what you have till I come' (2:25). Perhaps there is a hint of widespread gospel success to the church at Philadelphia — which would be kept 'from the hour of trial' (3:10) — in the promise that their persecutors would 'worship before [their] feet, and ... know that I have loved [them]' (v. 9).

The most notorious church that was in need of spiritual reviving was the church at Laodicea. These Christians were proud of their city, confident of their spirituality and ignorant of their real condition. The Spirit described them as 'lukewarm, and neither cold nor hot ... [you] do not know that you are wretched, miserable, poor, blind and naked' (3:16-17). They were counselled to seek God earnestly and in repentance in order to gain true spiritual wealth, holiness and enlightenment (gold, white garments and eye-salve). The picture here of Christ standing outside his church and pleading for admission, together with the promise of banqueting with his people, must refer to the radical contrast in their spiritual life before and after revival. I suggest that this is a clear invitation by the Lord of the church for them to come in repentance and plead with God for spiritual revival. For all the sermons that have been based on this letter to the church at Laodicea, the church today has not taken either its warnings or its promises seriously.

Perhaps the most intriguing fact about the letters to the seven churches is the nature of the promises that are offered to them. Most of the churches are offered promises that will clearly be fulfilled at the end of time. To Ephesus the promise of eating of 'the tree of life, which is in the midst of the paradise of God' (2:7) is apparently an end-of-time reward; which means that the only stated promise to this church is that God will not remove their witness (lampstand) so long as they repent (v. 5). The crown of life offered to the faithful at Smyrna (2:10) and the authority over the nations promised to Thyatira (2:26) may equally be end-time promises. The same can be said of the promises to Sardis (3:4-5). Yet at least three churches are given an expectation of a change in their circumstances here on earth. The Philadelphians will be kept from imminent persecution, and some of the other promises to them may have a fulfilment in their own day (3:9-10). The Laodiceans, of whom the Spirit had nothing positive to record, are offered the privilege of new spiritual life and the Lord returning to his church in an intimate friendship (3:18,20). It is a matter of debate how far the 'hidden manna' offered to Pergamum (2:17) is a spiritual refreshment rather than something only to be gained in the age to come. But in view of their confrontation with pagan feasts, it is very likely that the manna referred to here is the presence of the Lord himself among his people. I agree with Hendriksen who quotes favourably from Milligan, 'Those who overcome the temptation to participate in the heathen festivals and to eat food sacrificed to idols, shall be fed by the Lord himself: the grace of Christ and all its glorious fruits will be their food, invisible, spiritual, and hidden ... they receive the bread from heaven.[5]

Beyond the different circumstances and spiritual conditions of these churches lies the fact that the Spirit's offer of remedial action was also different. Some were told to repent and were offered new life in return; others were given no such offer of a refreshing. Some were in need of spiritual revival and were offered it — though the word 'revival' was not used. Others, like Smyrna, might have longed for just such a respite from their painful experience but were simply commanded to 'hold on'. All this reveals the sovereign Lord of the church dispensing to his people as he plans and not always as they might desire. What is clear is that most of these churches were being offered new life in return for the old — if they repented, corrected their failures and returned to the Lord. That is surely an offer of revival.

In summary, the possibility of any-time revival is more evident in the New Testament than is often appreciated. Pentecost is certainly understood as the fulfilment of Old Testament promises, and in that sense it is the greatest and most significant outpouring of the Spirit on the church. But it is not the last one. He came repeatedly upon the church in Jerusalem and elsewhere, and this was precisely what Peter prophesied during his sermon in Solomon's porch at the temple. Paul's prayers assumed the willingness of God to bless his church by the Spirit in almost inexpressible — because unimaginable — ways, and the promises of the Spirit to the churches in Asia towards the end of the first century were based equally upon the assumption that revival was a possibility following repentance. The clear expectation of the prophets throughout the old covenant is no less the anticipation of the apostles throughout the new.

7.
Praying for revival

To be convinced that revival is a thoroughly biblical experience which is found throughout both the Old and New Testaments, is only a first step — although a very important one. If, in the past, God has given his people this experience in their times of need, and if his character leads us to believe that it may be ours as often as we need it, plead for it, and he chooses to give it, then we are challenged to pray for it. But what does that mean in practice?

Hindrances to praying for revival

Today there are many reasons why Christians do not pray for revival. I examined some of these in *Revival! — a people saturated with God*. They included: opposition (revival is not a Christian experience), cynicism (overrated because it is overstated), doubt (a steady state is more biblical than a big bang), fear (its consequences are unpredictable) and discouragement (consistent disappointment reduces expectation). Over the past decade since I first wrote on the subject of revival, I have observed two other factors that have significantly confused prayer for revival. Both have already been referred to in this book.

The first is *misdirection*. Too often we have been led to believe that a particular contemporary experience is evidence of the wind of revival blowing. The experience has come, changed shape and either diminished or disappeared. But the assertion that this is revival has satisfied many. Sadly, too often a large section of professing Christians has been content with a stone instead of the Spirit. It is not unbelieving to be cautious before we assert that any particular phenomenon is the wind of revival. To claim too much too often leads either to general disillusion or to narrow satisfaction. We either give up in despair or we are content with anything. Either way, prayer for revival ceases. In his warning against Christians swallowing the culture of their day, J. I. Packer suggests that many evangelicals are 'restless existentialists'.[1] The constant demand for experiences to bolster our religion is a sad evidence of this.

The second addition concerns those who do pray for revival, and who do know what they mean by the term. However, this weakness causes significant confusion in prayer for revival. Although it may sound academic, I have called this an exegetical hindrance — or to be more precise it is *hermeneutical presumption.*[2] 'Hermeneutics' is the interpretation of a passage of Scripture: what it really means and how it should be applied. By adding the word 'presumption' I mean that Christians sincerely seeking revival often lay claims before God that are biblically unfounded. Some of the passages from the Bible that are commonly used in revival prayer meetings are misapplied; but from these passages we proceed to demand that God should keep his word. We have consequently used the Bible as a mantra, in the expectation that simply the recitation of Scripture must have persuasive force with God. But, as we have noted before, God is not committed to keep promises that he has not made.

To grasp the importance of this we must appreciate that there are two kinds of promise that God makes in Scripture: one is unconditional and specific and the other is conditional and either specific or general. In addition to this, God often reveals an aspect of his character that we can plead in prayer but he is not committed in advance to any specific response. The importance of this three-fold distinction is that if God does not keep his unconditional and specific promises then he ceases to be God, but he will not keep a conditional promise unless the conditions are fulfilled. On the other hand, if he does not respond according to our understanding of one aspect of his character we must assume that he has a higher and wiser purpose in view.

Let me give examples of each of these. God gave specific and unconditional promises concerning the ancestry of the Saviour of the world and of Israel's return from exile. Consequently, if the Messiah had not come through the line of Abraham and David, or if Israel had not returned to Jerusalem under Cyrus of Persia after her years of exile, then specific and unconditional promises of God would have failed. On the other hand, the promise in 2 Chronicles 7:14, 'If my people ... will humble themselves, and pray and seek my face...', is a conditioned promise that God gave to his chosen people Israel through Solomon; no specific occasion was in mind but a condition had to be fulfilled. Provided they responded sincerely to the condition, Israel could claim the promise whenever they were in need — and they often did. Because its fulfilment was not specifically located, how and when God responded would be wholly at his discretion.

This does not mean that 2 Chronicles 7:14 is out of bounds when the Christian prays for revival, because God reveals a principle about his own character in this verse. The 'land' referred to is the land of Israel, and no Christians in any nation today can claim this as a promise for their own land. But we may use this verse in our appeal to God, not on the ground of a specific promise he has made and must fulfil, or even on the ground of a conditional promise that he will keep providing we fulfil the conditions, but on the basis that this is a revelation of the kind of God he is: a forgiving and restoring God. In other words we can plead on the basis of the principle rather than

demand on the ground of a promise. God would still be a forgiving and restoring God if, for his better purposes, he did not
revive his people in response to their prayer. As an example of
prayer based upon the character of God, we may pray earnestly for the salvation of a friend or relation on the ground that
God is merciful; but he is not bound to answer as we request,
because mercy is only one aspect of his character.

In one Christian magazine a writer maintained, 'To release
faith for revival I must find the basis for my prayer in the promises of God.'[3] In this he is right, but we must be sure that the
areas of Scripture that we choose really are the promises of
God. In the same magazine another contributor refers us to
Matthew 13:24-43 and reasons that Christ's agricultural ana-
logies lead us to believe there will be days before the final Day
and harvests before the final Harvest at the end of the age. He
concludes, 'It seems to me beyond question that the world is
destined for a great and glorious revival in which multitudes
will be swept into the Kingdom of God.'[4] Doubtless that is his
wishful hope, but he offers no adequate New Testament evidence to support it. It is certainly not discovered in Matthew
13, and the only other passage referred to is Romans 11 which,
given the various interpretations of this chapter, can hardly be
held as a promise 'beyond question' of ultimate end-time revival. In other words, the writer is holding God to a promise
that he may never have made.

A third writer in this magazine comments on James 5:7-9
and 17-18, 'James implies that we ought to intercede for both
autumn and spring rains before the Lord's coming.'[5] But that
has nothing to do with James' intention. The farmer is an illustration of waiting patiently for the Second Coming of the Lord,
and Elijah is an illustration of praying in faith. Neither passage
can be taken as a promise of a specific coming revival. It is
hermeneutical presumption to suggest that a doctrine of periodic

revival leading to a great end-time revival can be built upon James 5:7. Similarly Acts 15:13-18 is taken as the basis for the hope that 'The world is destined for a great and glorious revival in which multitudes will be swept into the Kingdom of God.' The writer concludes that the use of Amos 9 in this passage is 'proof of a worldwide move of the Holy Spirit to gather men and women from every nation into the church of Jesus Christ.'[6] This is true in the sense of the steady work of the gospel throughout the history of the church, but in Acts 15 James simply uses Amos 9 to prove that God always intended to give the gospel to the elect Gentiles. To understand it as a specific promise of end-time revival is not an acceptable conclusion from Acts 15 or Amos 9. It is hermeneutical presumption.

This hermeneutical presumption has been widespread in the history of the church's longing for revival. When John Lorimer in the mid-nineteenth century used Luke 11:13, 'How much more will your Father in heaven give the Holy Spirit to those who ask him' (NIV) as a promise of end-time revival, he too had slipped into the same fallacy. I am not saying that Luke 11:13 cannot be used in prayer for revival, but simply that it cannot be held out to God as if it contains a specific promise of a specific period of revival at a specific time in the history of the church. What it does give us is the right to remind God of his character as a gracious and giving Father who wants the best for his children — and the best is giving his Holy Spirit to us. Lorimer claims, 'The Word of God teems with ... assurances and prophecies of a day of coming universal religious revival.'[7] But in this context the only references he offers us are Psalms 22 and 72; Isaiah 54:1 and Jeremiah 3:17. Such a conclusion would never be discovered in the passages themselves. This postmillennial approach has drawn a conclusion from an assumption that converts hermeneutics into presumption. Some have coined the word eisegesis to describe this. Exegesis is

reading the meaning out of the passage, whilst eisegesis is reading our own meaning into the passage.

None of this is intended to whittle away the value of Scripture in our prayer for revival; on the contrary, the Bible will
always remain our chief incentive and strongest plea with God
when praying for revival. However, we must be clear in our
minds whether our prayer is on the basis of God's unconditional
promise of specific revival, his conditional promise of revival
generally, or on the ground of what we know about his character as a revival-giving God. For example, seven centuries
before Pentecost the prophet Hosea had much to teach about
God's promise of revival to Israel, and this will strengthen our
resolve in prayer and add force to our hope to 'move the hand
that moves the world'. But Hosea 14:4-7 can never be
demanded from God today since it was a very specific promise
to Israel.

Having removed two significant barriers to effective prayer
for revival, we are ready to examine a few passages of Scripture that we may use in our prayerful longing for revival in our
own day. In the previous chapter we discovered just how large
the prayers and expectations of Paul were for the first-century
churches and concluded that if ever we do not know how to
pray as we should, those model prayers in Ephesians 1 and 3,
Colossians 1 and Philippians 1 would prove an excellent place
to begin. I often long to hear prayers that are grounded in Scripture. Here we will turn to the Old Testament.

What follows are not full expositions but are intended simply
as notes to put each passage in context and to highlight the
important themes. They are cameos of prayer for revival, which
could be used either privately or corporately as a preparation
for praying for revival. I have offered little close application.
This is deliberate, because I would hope that those who wish to
use these scriptures in ministry for prayer would work their own
application from the life of the church today.

Hosea 14:1-9 — Rejecting the methods of men

Here is a prayer offered on behalf of a people who have tried everything to improve their situation and now admit that God is their only solution.

After the death of Solomon (931 B.C.), civil war divided the nation into Israel in the north, based on the city of Samaria, and Judah in the south, based on Jerusalem. For two hundred years war alternating with uneasy peace characterized the relationship between the two nations. Hosea started his work earlier than the prophet Isaiah. He began preaching in the days of King Uzziah of Judah (810-758 B.C.) and continued for half a century or more. Jeroboam II of Israel led the north into a period of unprecedented prosperity (for some) and relative peace and security. The prophet Amos preached against Jeroboam's empty religion. After the king's death in 753 B.C., a quick succession of the remaining six kings in the north led to Assyrian domination and culminated in Israel withholding tribute from Assyria and forming an alliance with the broken reed of Egypt. In 722 B.C. Assyria invaded Samaria and carried the cream of the population into exile. This chapter is addressed to Israel, the northern kingdom, and the plea by Hosea for Israel to return in repentance apparently went unheeded in the north.

God has already been pleading with Israel

    Look at your sin (10:13)
    Look at your history (11:1-4)
    Look at your future (11:5-6)
    Look at your empty religion (11:7)
    Look at my affection for you (11:8)
    Look at the result of repenting or offending (13:1)
    Look at your 'security' (13:9-11)

Israel must acknowledge that their only help comes from God. He reminds them that they wanted to be like all the other nations and to use their methods — a king to go with them into battle and to govern the land.

In our own day we are driven by methods of commerce, social science or psychology. To suggest a return to the Lord by renewing the prayer meeting would be considered as too bland or simplistic. So, we struggle on in our own 'success', which we measure by numbers, programmes and buildings. We will attend any conference that offers a new method.

Here, then, is the prophet's plea:

> Take words and return to the Lord (14: 2-3). They were to take words, not just pious attitudes or wishful dreaming. In fact the prophet provides the words: an admission of guilt, a plea for mercy, a rejection of empty worship and an acknowledgement that their best schemes have failed them.

Then God responds by offering:

vv.4-7. a new spiritual life — their backsliding healed;
a new spiritual relationship — he will love them freely;
a new spiritual freedom — the anger of God turned away;
a new spiritual experience — God will be to them like dew
(during the dry season from March to October the nightmist provided sufficient moisture for life):
beauty (the lily) — Titus 2:10,
strength (cedars of Lebanon) — Ephesians 6:10,
royal honour (olive tree) — Revelation 1:6,
fragrance (cedars and the wine of Lebanon) — 2 Corinthians 2:15,
security (shadow of the cedars) — Romans 8:39,

> life (grain) — John 10:10,
> growth (the vine) — Ephesians 4:15,
> endurance (a green cypress tree) — 1 Corinthians 15:58,
> fruitfulness — Romans 7:4.

v.9   This is the way of wisdom! The plea may have passed
         unheeded by the north, but it was not without effect.
         Six years after the fall of Samaria, Hezekiah assumed
         the throne in Jerusalem and set himself to do all that
         Hosea had encouraged the northern kingdom to do —
         and revival followed (2 Chronicles 29 - 31).

For us, this passage does not provide the promise of revival
at any particular time, but it does lay out many of the principles
that we can apply to ourselves and many of the blessings that
we can interpret into a new covenant context. We are at liberty
to remind God of the way he dealt with his people in the Old
Testament — providing we are prepared to take notice of the
warnings, and correct our lives accordingly.

Isaiah 63:15 to 64:12 — Fulfilment beyond the present generation

To take this chapter on its own is to take it away from Scripture.
Isaiah began his ministry 'In the year that King Uzziah died'
(6:1; *c.*758 B.C.) and continued into the reign of Hezekiah — a
period of at least forty years. He was therefore a contemporary
of Hosea, but unlike Hosea who preached mainly to Israel,
Isaiah's message ranged widely and, in addition to Judah, he
prophesied against Israel in the north and most of the surrounding nations: Assyria, Babylon, Philistia, Moab, Syria, Ethiopia,
Egypt, Edom, Arabia and Tyre. It is doubtful whether any of
these responded; in fact the prophecies against them were more
for the benefit of Judah than for the nations concerned. The

prosperity under Jeroboam II in the north was matched under Uzziah in the south, with the same spiritual consequences. With the fall of Samaria in 722 B.C. Isaiah warned Jerusalem not to enter into alliances against Assyria and pleaded with the nation to return to God. The prophet lived through the period of revival in the time of Hezekiah (2 Chronicles 29 - 31) and played a significant role in the refusal of Hezekiah and Jerusalem to capitulate to Sennacherib of Assyria (Isaiah 36 - 37).

The plea of chapter 64 must be referring to events beyond the days of Hezekiah and therefore represents a longing for God to do again what he did in the time of that king. Isaiah lived on into the time of Hezekiah's son, Manasseh, whose reign of wickedness continued for half a century until most of his father's achievements had been reversed. Clearly the prophet is speaking against the background of a ruined city of Jerusalem (vv. 10-11). But there was no wholesale destruction of Jerusalem until the time of Nebuchadnezzar of Babylon in 587 B.C. — one hundred and seventy years after Isaiah began his ministry! Therefore Isaiah is looking forward prophetically to something he himself will never live to see. But in declaring the destruction of the cities of Judah, the city of Jerusalem and, most terrible of all, the temple itself (vv. 10-11), he is also aware of the restoration of the city. However, in his mind, the prophet moves beyond the restoration of the city and temple in the time of Ezra and Nehemiah to the creation of 'new heavens and a new earth' (65:17). From this point onward the whole picture is beyond earthly Zion and passes to and through the gospel age into the final act of God in history. Calvin sees this reference to the new heaven and new earth as 'exaggerated modes of expression to refer to the gospel age of the coming Messiah. But he continues, 'Nor does he mean only the first coming, but the whole reign, which must be extended as far as to the last coming'.[8] On the well-known passage of the wolf and the lamb (65:25 cf. 11:6-9) Calvin concludes, 'Beyond all controversy the Prophet speaks allegorically of bloody and violent men, whose cruel and savage nature shall be subdued, when they submit to the yoke of Christ.'[9] E. J. Young says much the same thing, 'In the concept of the prophet, time and eternity, the age of the New testament and the eternal heaven, are not sharply distinguished.'[10]

In the light of this, what do we expect when we follow this passage as a pattern-prayer for revival? Before we answer that, we should look at the verses themselves.

63:15-19. The ground upon which Isaiah takes his stand is that God sees all and must surely be concerned for the state of those who carry his honour in this world. The plea is based upon God's will ('your zeal'), his emotions ('the yearning of your heart'), and his relationship with his people ('you are our Father ... our Redeemer'). Boldly the prophet accuses God of inaction, as a result of which his servants have been hardened and have become indistinguishable from those who have never been God's special people. There is a daring courage about the way the prophet addresses God in his prayer, which would be arrogant presumption if it did not come from a man who had been through the humbling experience of chapter 6. It is a prayer that challenges God to act.

64:1-3. Isaiah is pleading for a miracle. This is evident from his poetry. Mixing his metaphors, he longs for an awesome revelation of divine power that would be like shaking mountains (as God did on Sinai) as easily as fire burns brushwood or boils water. Such an intervention would make both the name and presence of God known and revered among the nations.

64:4-7. The prophet has no doubt where the fault lies. After all, Jerusalem's God is the only true God and he is always ready to help those who rely on him, find their joy in him and who walk in righteousness. But God has good reason to be angry with his people, who continue to walk in their sinful disobedience. Isaiah confesses that he and the people are like filthy rags, and are tossed about like a dead leaf in the wind; no one cries out to God or clings desperately to him. Therefore their perilous state is all that they deserve.

64:8-12. The only claim that Isaiah can make upon God is that he represents the people whom God adopted and moulded for his use. Tragically, this claim appears incongruous in the light of the state of the city of Jerusalem — a desolate wilderness. All that was good is now ruined. In the light of this how can God hold back from coming to help his people?

In the chapter that follows God adds to the desperate picture by underscoring their sin which was their only response to his grace. But in promising better times ahead, it is not for the present generation, who have neglected God's repeated plea to return to him, but for their descendants (65:9-10). The fact that the prophecy is looking forward to the coming of the Messiah is clear from verses 13-16 and the reference to a people called 'by another name'. From here Isaiah moved immediately into the promise of 'new heavens and a new earth' (vv. 17-25).

How then can we use chapter 64 as a prayer for revival? Simply because that is exactly what Isaiah was longing for. The cause and ground of his prayer, and what he requested, is precisely the same for the church today. The fact that the answer lay in the distant future does not alter the reality of the prayer or, for that matter, the fulfilment. God will respond with such a supernatural intervention that the whole world will be shaken as fire burns brushwood and boils water. He will do this with the coming of the Messiah. In a similar way, in 64:4 Isaiah was doubtless looking back at God's previous acts of grace for his people, but when the apostle Paul read that passage he applied it to the time of the gospel (1 Corinthians 2:9). In other words the principle could go either way! So, the prayer is a valid, bold and heartfelt plea for revival, irrespective of how God actually fulfilled Isaiah's petition.

Jeremiah 14:7-9,19-22 — A people deceived by promises of peace and prosperity

Jeremiah's ministry covered almost half a century from 626 B.C. to the fall of Jerusalem in 587 B.C. and possibly beyond. He preached through the reigns of five kings in Judah, from Josiah to Zedekiah. Brought up in a priestly home, Jeremiah was called to his ministry as a young man at the beginning of the reforms of Josiah. In fact, Jeremiah's early preaching probably significantly contributed to Josiah's zeal, together with the rediscovery of the law of God. However, with the untimely death of the king in battle, Jeremiah found himself among a backsliding people who were ripe for judgement. Frequently he stood alone, warning of judgement whilst the false prophets assured the nation that all would be well. He suffered severely for this, particularly during the time of the Babylonian siege of Jerusalem. Although Jeremiah was an uncompromising preacher of judgement, he was also the prophet who assured the nation that their suffering and exile would not last for ever, and that a return and restoration would follow.

The prophecies recorded in Jeremiah are not all in chronological order, though it is fairly safe to say that this passage belongs to the time of Josiah. Manasseh and his son Amon had left the nation in a terrible state. The half century of Manasseh's evil reign was hardly improved even after his repentance at the close of his life, and Amon continued the same spiritual slide. Josiah came to the throne at the age of eight and at the age of sixteen he set himself to seek the Lord; in the twelfth year of his reign the king began his reforms (2 Chronicles 34:1-3). Significantly it was a year later that Jeremiah commenced his own ministry (Jeremiah 1:1-2) though it was not until another five years had passed that the law was rediscovered in the temple (2 Chronicles 34:14). Jeremiah 14:19-22 must be seen then, not in the light of Josiah's early reforms, but in the light of the many decades of decadence that preceded Josiah. Reform is not the same as revival and Jeremiah's great complaint was that there appeared to be little change of heart among the people. They were content simply to do the right things.

14:7-9.   The people were suffering a period of severe drought as a punishment for their 'backslidings' and the prophet's plea is a cry for rain. He acknowledged the nation's sin and his bitter regret was the paradox that although the LORD was 'in our midst', he appeared to be nothing more than a passing traveller in the land; unknown even to his own people. The desperate plea, 'Do not leave us!', came from a man who knew the bitter consequences of God walking away from his own people. In fact, God responded by saying that since they have wandered from him, he would no longer listen to them or take notice of their empty ritual (vv. 10-12). Unfortunately Jeremiah was not the only preacher in his day; others were holding out the promise of peace and prosperity that led the people into a false security that all was well. Did not the current reforms indicate that?

14:19-20.   The warning of 'sword and famine' led Jeremiah to pour out one of his most powerful prayers on record.

He has a cluster of strong words to describe how he believes the people have been treated by God: rejected, loathed, chastised, dismayed, spurned and treated with contempt. In fact, contrary to the promises of the false prophets, there was no healing, no peace, nothing agreeable. But the prophet turned these descriptions into questions because they appeared to be inconsistent with all the promises of God: Have you? Why have you? However, Jeremiah knew only too well that whilst God's ultimate promise to his people was unconditional, it did not mean that they would not be punished for bad behaviour (see, for example, 2 Samuel 7:13-16). Therefore, without waiting for an answer, Jeremiah confessed their 'wickedness, iniquity and sin'. It is wildly dangerous to tolerate sloppy and sinful activity by placing our confidence in 'evidence' that God is with us.

14:21-22. Then followed the only claim the prophet could make upon God. There were no excuses, only a hope that God would act for his own sake, that he would recognize that in the disgrace of his people was his own disgrace and that he had a covenant commitment to the people. Besides, where else could he go? None of the idols of the surrounding nations could produce rain — of that there was no doubt. He alone was their LORD and God. In the light of all this, Jeremiah was determined to 'wait' for God — a word that means to look eagerly and hopefully for something.

Although Jeremiah was pleading for rain, it was not rain above all that we wanted. He recognized that the real need was far bigger than this. The absence of rain was the result of their persistent disobedience in listening to the false prophets and relying upon their daily worship ritual. Only a spiritual revival could turn the hand of God for them instead of against them.

Once again we have a prayer that must be understood before it is used. There are close applications to be made to the life of our churches today and it may be painful to turn the finger of God through Jeremiah against ourselves — but it must be done. The parallels may be obvious with a moment of thought, and God will no more respond to the self-satisfaction of his people today than he did then. Whatever our equivalent of 'rain', we should learn from the prophet that that is not be our greatest need.

Daniel 9:4-19 — A model prayer for revival

The unbroken succession of the prophets continues. Daniel was a teenager when he was take into exile in Babylon in the year 587 B.C. As Jeremiah came to the close of his ministry, Daniel was at the threshold of his own. As with Jeremiah, the chapters in the Book of Daniel are not in strict chronological order, but by the time of this prayer, Daniel was an old man of around eighty years who had maintained his integrity of life and faith under six pagan and despotic rulers. In his regular, daily time of prayer, he had been reading in the prophet Jeremiah. Sadly, many of the sins that caused the people to be taken into exile had stayed with them, and in Daniel's prayer we can hear the same urgent cry that we have found in Hosea, Isaiah and Jeremiah. Daniel, like all the prophets, prayed in the first person plural 'we'. It is identification with the people. The prophets do not pray 'for them' but 'from us'. In preaching they speak on behalf of God to the people and therefore they point the finger and condemn the sins. In prayer they speak on behalf of the people to God and therefore they plead for forgiveness and confess the sins.

v.2.   His prayer was based upon the promises of God
               — Jeremiah 29:10-14,

v.4.   and upon the character of God — great, awesome,
               covenant-keeping and merciful.

vv.5-6.   His confession was focused — sin, iniquity,
               wickedness, rebellion, transgression,
               disobedience,

vv.7-8.   and the results were understood — shame and
               disgrace.

vv.11-14.   Daniel accepted that the punishment was just —
               as Moses warned and because the Lord is
               righteous.

v.12.   The disaster is great — there had been nothing like
               it before.

v.16.   But there is a covenant claim — we are a special
               people,

vv.17-19.   more particularly the honour of God is at stake —
               'for your own sake' and 'for the sake of your name',
               your mercy is great.

v.19.   There is an urgency — hear, forgive, act.

Did God respond?

               More than half a century earlier, God looked for
               someone to stand before him in prayer on behalf
               of the nation (Ezekiel 22:30). He found no one, so
               the judgement fell. Daniel was a teenager then but
               he is now determined to stand in the gap. Did God
               hear and respond? The answer is found in
               2 Chronicles 36:22-23.

Psalm 44 — Dishonour when we have tried to be faithful

Here is a very different cause for prayer from all that we have seen so far. A people who humbly believe that they have done all they can to please God yet discover that there is still no sign that God is with them. Here is a psalm that Charles Grandison Finney probably never discovered or else, in the light of it, he would have been compelled to revise his theology. Often, as in the time of Hosea, Isaiah, Jeremiah and Daniel, we can identify the sin that is the cause of our spiritual ill health and the consequent dishonour brought upon God; but sometimes we are mystified at our apparent neglect by God! It is not that we claim to be perfect, but we have sincerely tried to please him in every way.

A summary of the psalm reveals the writer's perplexity: you have helped us; we still boast about you helping us; but you are not helping us; so you must help us.

We do not know who wrote this psalm or on what occasion. It forms a trio with Psalms 42 and 43 where the psalmist longs for God in his discouragement and yearns for the time when he can yet again worship at Jerusalem. The references in Psalm 44 to being scattered among the nations (v. 11) and the mocking derision of the nations (v. 14) would indicate some time in the exile; this would make it contemporaneous with Daniel.[11] If this is so, we have discovered another small group of faithful Jews in the land of exile. The title 'of the sons of Korah' would imply that singing was one way the exiles encouraged one another, since the descendants of Korah were the temple musicians. However, what is without a doubt is the theme.

The psalmist's promise of loyalty

vv.1-3.   Singing was not the only way that the faithful encouraged one another. They read the stories of God's

great deliverance in the past, and in doing so acknowledged that victory did not belong to the nation, but
to God alone. Clearly the psalmist, and those he
represents, found great delight in reading the history
of God's dealing with his people and admired the
times when the people were faithful.

vv.4-8.   But the psalmist insisted that it was no different with
him and his people. They also sincerely claimed God
to be their King and they would not trust in themselves. They constantly boasted that God alone was
their hope and all their trust was in him. In the past
they had proved this, and they were still not ashamed
to claim it — in spite of all the appearances to the
contrary.

v.17.   They had not forgotten God and they had tried to
live as his covenant people should live. They had
kept their heart intent on pleasing him and had
walked according to his Word.

vv.20-21.   If all this is hypocrisy and a sham, God would know
because no secret can be hidden from him.

The psalmist's protest of neglect

He addresses God directly. In spite of all their
endeavours:

vv.9-12.   You appear to have abandoned us and all our best
efforts to serve you come to nothing. We achieve
little, and often go backward instead of forward. You
gain nothing by our lack of success but still you do
not take action to help us.

vv.13-16,19,22. Those around us laugh and despise us. The world shakes its head in pity. They see us as yesterday's men and women. We cannot escape their constant mocking, and instead of us spoiling the world, the world spoils us. Every day we are like food for jackals and sheep for slaughter.

The psalmist's prayer for help

vv.23-24.   Can it be that you are asleep to our desperate need?
Have you cast us away from your love for ever?
Why do you hide your face from us?
Why do you forget your own people in their affliction?

v.25.   We can hardly go any lower than we are.

v.26.   Lord, it is time to stir yourself so that people will honour you as a God of mercy.

The boldness of the psalmist is staggering. He dares to suggest to God, 'We have not forgotten you, but you appear to have forgotten us; we talk of you all day long, but you seem to be asleep.' To offer such a prayer is arrogant presumption unless we are certain that God himself would approve of the claims we make about ourselves. God wants his people to be bold with him, but never presumptuous and never arrogant. Certainly we can pray as the psalmist prayed, but only when our promise of loyalty is as convincing as his.

Psalm 77 — I cannot allow myself to be discouraged

The theme of this psalm is not too dissimilar from Psalm 44 except that that was a corporate psalm — the 'we' and 'us' were predominant — whereas this one is intensely personal. The psalmist is alone with his problem. It is a model of the way in which we may counsel ourselves when we are discouraged. How to lift ourselves up when we are cast down is a lost art among many Christians today; we prefer to run to the counsellor instead. We are told who wrote this psalm. Asaph was chief choirmaster under King David and his instrument was the cymbals (1 Chronicles 16:4-5). Two hundred years later Asaph's psalms, and those of David, formed the songbook of revival in the time of Hezekiah (2 Chronicles 29:30). What was the cause of his despair we do not know, but it is commonplace for Christians today to feel overwhelmed by the hardness of people's hearts and their strong opposition to the gospel. When our best efforts come to nothing, and at times even God himself seems to be a long way off, there is always the temptation to give up. Asaph has left us a wise example.

v.1.   Before he plunges into despair, our psalmist establishes at least this much: 'When I cried out, God heard me.' If all else seemed to be against him, that much he would never doubt. It was his one firm constant. God is listening out for his people.

vv.2-3.   Such was his despair that it seemed as if his very soul refused to accept comfort, and even thinking about God and calling out to him made his circumstances all the more inexplicable. But he was certain of this: he would go to God with his complaining, and to no one else.

vv.4-6.   The psalmist could not sleep, so he allowed his mind to be distracted from its present anxiety by thinking of past blessings from God. Blessings that were not just towards himself, but which God had sent in years long past. Diligently he ransacked the history of

God's providence to remind himself of the glorious interventions of God.

vv.7-9.   Unfortunately that initially had the opposite effect of his intentions. It appeared that:
God no longer did what he used to do;
his once gracious mercy had now ceased;
his promises had run dry and had failed;
he had even forgotten to be gracious ever again;
he was relentlessly angry.

v.10.   Well, that is exactly how the psalmist felt. The years of God's right hand of favour and grace in the past only showed up the present in black contrast and caused a deeper distress.

vv.11-15. Nevertheless — and this is the psalmist's secret — he will persist not only in recalling God's great deeds in the past, but will also think about them and talk about them. In that way he will encourage others and be encouraged himself. He will become more and more convinced of the reality of God's mercy, the necessity of his mercy and the possibility of his mercy.

vv.16-20. He seems not to have progressed beyond Moses in his recollection of history! The parting of the great rivers and the awesome events of Sinai were enough to convince him that although God's footprints are not always seen, they are always there; and that although Moses and Aaron may not always have made a good job of their leadership God was, after all, the great Shepherd.

The psalm ends at this point! Perhaps he had resolved his problem by now and was settled in the conviction that the absence of God was more apparent than real; and that all the negatives that seemed so real would evaporate in the light of true reality (vv. 7-9).

Spurgeon comments on this psalm, 'It has much sadness in it, but we may be sure it will end well, for it begins with prayer, and prayer never has an ill issue.' It is true that reflecting on the past great deeds of God may at times only compound our confusion, but that is no bad thing if it drives us more fervently to God. We seem to be so far from the possibility of God changing the condition of our churches and our society, and what God has done in the past is hard to imagine for our present circumstances. In fact, he does not seem to act in that way any more. These thoughts can easily depress us unless we learn from Asaph. Far from abandoning his reading of the history of salvation, it only compelled him to look closer and deeper into the story of God's great activity for his people. As he did so, his heart became more and more convinced that God is God alone and all hope belongs to him. Once begun, Asaph continued his reading, and Psalm 78 expands the theme. If we long for revival in our day, we must never allow a generation to grow up in ignorance of the footprints of God.

Psalm 85 — Again, Lord!

This psalm is different again. Unlike Psalms 44 or 77, the psalmist seems to have lived through a time of revival and he therefore knows from personal experience what that means. It is another psalm from the descendants of Korah. Since there is a reference to the LORD having brought his people back from captivity (v. 1) we could place it during the time of Ezra-Nehemiah when, after the decree of Cyrus, the early zeal of the return had settled to a cold routine. But this is not certain, Spurgeon, typically, adamantly attributes it to David; at a time when the land was oppressed by the Philistines. Leupold suggests shortly after the return from the Babylonian captivity. Calvin, with no compelling reason, believes it was composed 'to be sung by the people when they were persecuted by the cruel tyranny of Antiochus' — presumably he meant Antiochus IV which would place it a little earlier than his suggestion for Psalm 44. I would go with Leupold as the most probable. The prophets Haggai and Zechariah were sent to challenge the returned exiles to a new zeal and perhaps this lament was composed at the same time; evidently singing was a significant part of the people's worship (Nehemiah 12:45-47).

vv.1-3.   The 'you have' — repeated six times — took place at the return from exile, and our psalmist was there. The people's response at that time is recorded in Ezra 3.

vv.4-7.   Clearly the spiritual life of the nation is flagging. The psalmist plays on the same word that he has used of God in verse 3, as God 'turned back' from the fierceness of his anger so they need to be 'turned back' to him ('restore' in verse 4 is the same word). With good reason God has turned away from them. This could have been when the people did not persist in their efforts to rebuild the temple (Ezra 4) or later when Nehemiah drew attention to necessary reforms (Nehemiah 13). The consequence of their disobedience was that their joy in God and their experience of salvation had evaporated. The psalmist presents God with a choice, 'Will you (repeated) be angry always, or will you revive us?' The word used here means 'quicken, refresh, restore, revive'. It has to do with new life. He longs for their joy to be restored as the people are revived. The Puritan Thomas Watson said, 'God has no design upon us, but to make us happy', and Spurgeon comments on verse 6, 'God loves to see his children happy.' But each meant happiness found in God. Revival is one of the best ways by which God can make his people happy.

vv. 8-9.   The fearful questions in verse 5 were clearly rhetorical since the psalmist is confident of the outcome: he will again hear the Lord speaking peace to the people. However, it can all quickly be lost if they do not firmly resist the temptation to slide back into folly. The psalmist has a clear priority in his mind. 'Glory' is the presence of God known and felt among the people. That is not only for *their* enjoyment, but also for God's own honour.

vv. 10-13. Here is the final blend of the past and the future. In the past, when the nation followed God, both mercy and truth met each other and righteousness and peace kissed. God's mercy and peace will always accompany truth and righteousness. But here, the righteousness is from heaven — it is the Lord giving what is good in response to truth springing up from the earth to meet him. The good that he will give to his people and do for them (righteousness) will go ahead of them and, unlike the psalmist in Psalm 77, they will see his footsteps clearly and will make *that* their pathway.

Prayer as meaning or mantra

Given that we believe in the necessity and the possibility of revival, most Christians will acknowledge the importance of prayer. But acknowledgement and action are often a world apart. A cursory request for revival, even repeated daily, is hardly the same as a heart-cry for God to take action in defence of his name and his honour. There are few prayer meetings today that are wholly committed to revival, and even fewer that take seriously the need to present a reasoned and responsive case before God. Prayer, any prayer, is not simply a matter of letting God hear our voice. If we are serious about obtaining what we most long for, we must be sure of the ground on which we come; do we have a biblical case to present to him? This is what I mean by a 'reasoned' case. But we must also be ready to respond in whatever way his Word directs. The prophets knew that the people must put things right if they were to expect a response from God.

God listens to prayers, not mantras (Matthew 6:7). Simply to quote Scripture passages to God is no guarantee that they are relevant to our cause, still less that he will listen and respond. There is no value in using just any passage of Scripture in prayer until it becomes a mantra for revival. We must understand firstly whether the passage, taken in its context, is relevant to our subject and secondly what we mean by each turn of phrase. The Bible is to be understood not just quoted — and applied not just believed. To think through each passage before we use it, to place it in its context and then to apply it to our own situation, is the only way to call God to attention and press our case for revival.

How can we encourage prayer for revival? There is probably no such thing as a typical prayer meeting, but to commence with a corporate act of worship focusing upon the Triune

God (and not our own experiences) can never be misplaced. A brief introduction to an historical revival (or aspect of revival) establishes the thing we are longing for and reminds everyone of the historical reality of our subject. But it is essential that a passage of Scripture should be read and explained, in a way similar to the examples above. In this way we may be driven to prayer not simply by the desperate state of our society or our church, but by the encouragement of Scripture. God will respond to his people when their hearts are right, their minds informed, their lives consistent and their cause good. There is no better way to ensure all of these than by placing ourselves under the instruction and incentive of Scripture.

But all this is hard work! It means we can no longer idly toss Bible passages towards heaven on the assumption that our intention is what matters. God expects his people to handle his Word with care, and that means with thought. Perhaps, after all, it is not just our sin that stands in the way of God pouring out his Spirit in revival, but our ignorance of that tool which he has placed into our hands to persuade him.

If we have come this far in general agreement in our study of a theology of revival, then we should have gained a determination to seek God through intelligent and persistent prayer. Such a response can only be healthy for his people. If the church today assailed heaven for the right thing, to the right end and with the right reasons then we could expect to see God respond. I do not mean that we could anticipate inevitable revival, that much should be clear by now, but I do believe that such diligent searching for God will always bring blessing to his people.

Two opposite dangers confront us at the end of any study on the subject of revival. On the one hand, we may decide that revival is not for the church today because the day of grace has passed and things can only get worse — in consequence we do nothing. On the other hand, we may conclude that until God comes in revival there is no hope for the unbelief of the world or the backsliding of the church — and in consequence we do nothing!

I have nothing new to say in response to this, but the matter is so important that I will borrow the words with which I closed my first book on revival, 'However much we may be convinced of the biblical nature of revival and of the urgency of our need and the benefit it would bring, nothing must be allowed to hinder our work in the 'ordinary times'. Our life of prayer, our striving for holiness, and our wholehearted evangelism must all go on as if the future of the church of Christ depended upon them. At the same time we should long for our community to be 'saturated with God', we ought often to be talking of the great acts of God in revival and our prayers should continually remind God that we need a 'special occasion' for this generation.'[12]

Is revival then the only hope of the church of Christ? I do not believe so. Across the world there are serious and faithful congregations with a deep love for Christ, worshipping and working together in harmony and love, there are Christian leaders of impeccable character leading their people in spiritual wisdom, and there are gospel preachers who loyally and without fear proclaim nothing but the truth of God's Word. This, together with the guarantee of our Saviour, is the hope for the future growth of the church. My understanding of the Scriptures leads me to the conclusion that however glorious revival is and however much it increases the numerical and spiritual vigour of the church, it is not essential to the growth and existence of the church worldwide. I do not even believe that revival is the church's finest hour! During the second and third centuries of the church thousands of Christians, both men and women, were brutally tortured and gruesomely martyred for their refusal to deny the Saviour who had died for them, and they were not all living in times of revival. Those where some of the finest days of the history of the church. Ever since then to the present day there has been a stream of martyrs for Christ — on some estimates there are currently more than 160,000 each year. The church in the fires of persecution is so often the church at her finest.

This may be an unexpected ending to such a study as this, but however much I long for and believe in revival, I am convinced that those who are first in the Kingdom of God are not necessarily those who lived during times of spiritual revival, but those who persevered when all around seemed to give way. Soldiers prove themselves on the rugged terrain in the face of a vigorous and vicious enemy, not on the quiet beaches of a tropical paradise. More honours are won by the soldiers who maintain their morale and courage when the tide of battle is running against them than in the heady days of victory.

To repeat what we said in the introduction to this book, we must learn to be a people satisfied with God even when we are not yet saturated with God. A satisfied dissatisfaction is one of those necessary paradoxes of the Christian life. Besides, revival should never be the all-consuming concern of the church. Good things can happen for the church and through the church even on the outside of revival. We can only conclude with the prophet Micah, 'Therefore I will look to the LORD; I will wait for the God of my salvation; my God will hear me' (Micah 7:7).

Notes

Introduction
1. Published by Evangelical Press, 1990.
2. Iain H. Murray, *Pentecost – Today?,* Banner of Truth, 1998, p.5-6.
3. *Revivals of Religion - Lectures by Charles Grandison Finney.* Ed. With notes by William Henry Harding. Marshall, Morgan and Scott, 1913, p.33-4. More accessible for today's reader is an edited edition by Bethany House Publishers, Minneapolis, 1988. However, my references are to the older edition.
4. *Ibid.,* p.49. Especially see Lecture 8 where he has some helpful advice for those who lead a prayer meeting.
5. See *Finney's Lectures on Theology,* Eerdmans, 1953. The lectures were originally given to the students at Oberlin College in America in 1846. The first publication in England was in 1851.
6. *Ibid.,* p.326.
7. *Ibid.,* p.397.
8. *Revivals of religion - Lectures by Charles Grandison Finney,* p.196-7.
9. William B. Sprague, *Lectures on Revivals of Religion,* Banner of Truth, 1959, p.102.
10. *Ibid.,* p.112.
11. *Ibid.,* p.105.
12. *Revivals of Religion - Lectures by Charles Grandison Finney,* p.6.
13. *Ibid.,* p.29.
14. *Ibid.,* p.5.
15. J. F. Thornbury, *God Sent Revival,* Evangelical Press, 1977, p.227.
16. For an excellent critique of Finney and the issues see Iain H. Murray, *Revival and Revivalism,* Banner of Truth, 1994.
17. The best contemporary record of the origins of this revival that led to the conversion of possibly one million people in America is found in Samuel Prime's *The Power of Prayer,* Banner of Truth, 1991. Originally it was published in 1859 and Finney was quite disparaging of it.
18. Published by Inter-Varsity and Paternoster, 1979, p.243.
19. It was reprinted in 1993 by The Reformed Book Outlet, Hudsonville, Michigan, USA.
20. See also Frank Bartleman, *How Pentecost Came to Los Angeles,* first published in 1925, reprinted as *Azusa Street* in 1980.

21. *Revival! - a people saturated with God*, p.210 ff.
22. Erroll Hulse, *Give Him No Rest*, Evangelical Press, 1991, pp.18-20.
23. *Revivals of Religion*, p.22.
24. Murray, *Pentecost Today?*, p.5.
25. James I. Packer, *God in our Midst*, pp.10-11.

Chapter 1 — 'The Holy Spirit in the Old Testament'
1. John H. Armstrong, *When God Moves*, Harvest House Publishers, 1998, p.43.
2. Murray, *Pentecost Today*, p.14 quoting from Sinclair Ferguson, *The Holy Spirit*, IVP (Illinois), 1996, p.26.
3. Ferguson, *ibid.*, pp.24-5.
4. Charles Ryrie, *Dispensationalism Today*, Moody Press, 1965, p.44. On the other hand, George Smeaton in his study, *The Doctrine of the Holy Spirit*, reprinted by Banner of Truth, 1958, p.44, asserts that by the power of the Spirit 'countless millions had been regenerated ... since the first promise in Eden.'
5. Murray, *Pentecost Today*, p.31.
6. Benjamin B. Warfield, *Biblical and Theological Studies*, Presbyterian and Reformed Publishing Company, 1952, p.134. See also Sinclair Ferguson in *The Holy Spirit*, pp.18-21, for a defence of the work of the Spirit at creation.
7. George T. Montague, *Holy Spirit – Growth of a Biblical Tradition*, Hendrikson Publishers Inc. (MA), 1976, p.57. This is a useful book tracing the development of an understanding of the Spirit through the Bible. However, the author's commitment to a form critical view of the canon means that his chronological development is suspect. For example, Kings comes before Numbers and Paul before Matthew!
8. *Ibid.*, pp.57-8.
9. Warfield, *Biblical and Theological Studies*, p.138.
10. *The Works of John Owen*, Banner of Truth, 1965, Vol. 3, p.151.
11. Quoted in Montague, p.114.
12. *Ibid.* pp.116-24.
13. Smeaton, *The Doctrine of the Holy Spirit*, p.37.
14. Ferguson, *The Holy Spirit*, p.24-5.
15. Smeaton, *The Doctrine of the Holy Spirit*, p.27.
16. Meredith G. Kline, *Images of the Spirit*, private publication, 1980.
17. *Ibid.*, p.45.
18. *Ibid.*, p.69. On page 70 he refers to it as 'The Old Testament version of Pentecost'.
19. Smeaton, *The Doctrine of the Holy Spirit*, p.40.
20. Warfield, *Biblical and Theological Studies*, p.128.
21. Ferguson, *The Holy Spirit*, pp.25-6.
22. Smeaton, *The Doctrine of the Holy Spirit*, p.32.
23. Warfield, *Biblical and Theological Studies*, p.128.
24. *Ibid.*, pp.151-2.
25. *Ibid.*, p.127.
26. James Montgomery Boice, *Foundations of the Christian Faith*, IVP, 1986, p.376.

Notes

27. Donald Guthrie, *New Testament Theology,* IVP, 1981, p.513.
28. *Ibid.,* p.526.
29. Meredith Kline, *Images of the Spirit*, p.85.
30. *Ibid.,* p.94.
31. James B. Jordan, *Through New Eyes*, Wolgemuth and Hyatt, 1988, pp.138-40.

Chapter 2 — 'Examples of revival in the Old Testament'
1. Murray, *Pentecost – Today?*, p.16.
2. Keil and Delitzsch, *Commentary on the Old Testament,* Vol.1, p.120.
3. For example Calvin, Keil and Delitzsch, Leupold, and Morris.
4. Ron Davies, *I Will Pour Out My Spirit*, Monarch, 1992, p.44.
5. *Notes on the Hebrew Text of the Books of Samuel,* Oxford, Clarendon Press, p.61.
6. W. B. Sprague, *Lectures on Revival,* Banner of Truth, 1959, p.1.
7. Richard F. Lovelace, *Dynamics of Spiritual Life*, Inter-Varsity/Paternoster, 1979, p.61.

Chapter 4 — 'The expectation of revival in the Old Testament'
1. A useful introduction to the various views is *The Meaning of the Millennium,* Inter Varsity Press (USA), 1980.
2. John Murray, and see the views of Iain H. Murray in *The Puritan Hope,* Banner of Truth, 1971.
3. *The Time is at Hand,* Presbyterian and Reformed Publishing Co., 1970, pp.7-11.
4. Edward J. Young, *The Book of Isaiah,* Vol. 2, Eerdmans, 1969.
5. Calvin *Commentaries,* Vol. 8, Baker Book House, 1979.
6. *Commentary on the Old Testament,* Vol. 7, Eerdmans, 1976.
7. Murray in *The Puritan Hope* presents the Puritan postmillennial position clearly.
8. Jonathan Edwards in *The History of Redemption* in *Works,* Vol. 1, Banner of Truth, 1974.
9. edited by W. M. Hetherington and republished by the Banner of Truth in 1984.
10. *Ibid.,* p.202.
11. Calvin Colton, *History and Character of American Revivals of Religion,* Westley and Davis, London, 1838, pp.141,195-6. Quoted in Lovelace, *Dynamics of Spiritual Life*, pp.401-2.
12. Quoted in Thornbury, *God Sent Revival,* pp.139-40.
13. A careful study of his life is found in Arnold Dallimore, *The Life of Edward Irvine*, Banner of Truth, 1983.
14. *More than Conquerors*, William Hendriksen, Baker Book House, 1939.
15. *Ibid.*, Preface.
16. *Restoration* for September/October, 1989.
17. Bryn Jones in *Revive Us Again,* Harvestime, 1990, p.20.
18. *Ibid.,* p.93.
19. The 'Beulah' meeting at Wembley on 16 October 1992.
20. *Restoration,* July/August 1989, p.24.

21. R. S. Rushdoony, *God's Plan for Victory,* Thorburn Press, Virginia, 1977.
22. Thornbury, *God Sent Revival*, pp.142-3.
23. *The Revival of Religion*, p.203.
24. *Ibid.*, p.214.
25. *Ibid.*, p.221.

Chapter 5 — 'The expectation of the Old Testament — a study of the Scriptures'

1. Alec Motyer, *The Prophecy of Isaiah*, IVP, 1993, pp.31-2.
2. *Ibid.*, p.29.
3. See Calvin's Commentary on Isaiah.
4. See Calvin on Acts of the Apostles.
5. Edward J. Young, *The Book of Isaiah,* Eerdmans, 1977, vol. 3, p.448.
6. *The Minor Prophets,* Concordia Publishing House, 1970, pp.125-6.
7. R. E. Davies, *I will pour out my Spirit*, Monarch, 1992, p.44.

Chapter 6 — 'The New Testament expectation of revival'

1. *Revival! – a people saturated with God,* p.231.
2. See Moulton and Milligan, *Vocabulary of the Greek New Testament,* Hendrickson Publishers, Oct 1997 (orig. one vol. ed., 1930).
3. It is the form known as the second aorist subjunctive.
4. For example 'the 38th year of the dominion of Caesar, son of the god'. Moulton and Milligan, *Vocabulary of the Greek New Testament.*
5. Milligan, Th*e Book of Revelation,* 1889, p.265 quoted in *More than Conquerors,* Baker Book House, 1958, p.84.

Chapter 7 — 'Praying for revival'

1. J. I. Packer, *A Quest for Godliness*, Crossway, Illinois, p.30.
2. In a different context, but on the same theme of misapplying Scripture, Don Carson refers to 'exegetical fallacies' in his book under that title (Baker, 1996) – a book that every preacher would do well to read.
3. Bryn Jones, *Restoration* Sept/Oct, 1989, p.20.
4. Tony Ling, *ibid.,* p.18.
5. Hugh Thompson, *ibid.,* p.16-17.
6. Tony Ling, *ibid.,* p.19.
7. *The Revival of Religion* edited by W. M. Hetherington and republished by the Banner of Truth in 1984, p.188.
8. Calvin on Isaiah, Baker, 1979, p.398.
9. *Ibid.,* p.406.
10. *The Book of Isaiah,* Eerdmans, 1972, p.514.
11. Leupold puts it in the time of David (900 B.C.), though even Spurgeon is not sure about this, and Calvin places it in the time of the Maccabees (150 B.C.). So, who knows?
12. In *Revival! – a people saturated with God*, I gave over a whole chapter to 'Our response to revival', pp.227-40.

Scripture index

Other books by Brian Edwards published by Evangelical Press:

God's outlaw — William Tyndale and the first printed New Testament in English
Not by chance — making sense out of suffering
Nothing but the truth — the inspiration, authority and reliability of the Bible
Revival! — *a people saturated with God*
Shall we dance? — the role of dance and drama in worship and evangelism
Through many dangers — the story of John Newton

Other books by Brian Edwards published by Day One Publications:

AD — a full-colour booklet to celebrate the millennium, describing the impact of the Bible on British society from the time the gospel first entered Britain
Horizons of hope — *reality in disability* (eight stories of coping with disability, including Brian and Barbara's story)
In conversation booklets — a series dealing with a range of issues facing Christians today
No longer two — a guide to Christian engagement and marriage
The Ten Commandments for today — a commentary, applying the Ten Commandments to contemporary society

Symposiums edited by Brian Edwards and published by Day One Publications as part of the *Facing the issue* series:
Men, women and authority
Homosexuality today — *the straight agenda*

A selection of books by
Brian H. Edwards
published by
Evangelical Press

Revival! — A people saturated with God
Large paperback, 304pp
ISBN 0-85234-273-X
Published by Evangelical Press

It was the week-night prayer meeting. There had been bitter opposition to the gospel in the village, and although many attended the meetings from other areas, very few locals attended. A church leader suggested they should go to prayer, and thirty or so moved into the home of a friendly farmer. Prayer was heard, and about midnight Duncan Campbell turned to the local blacksmith, who had been silent so far, and said, 'I feel the time has come when you ought to pray.' The man prayed for about half an hour, 'because in revival time doesn't matter', and then drew his prayer to a close with a bold challenge: 'God, do you not know that your honour is at stake? You promised to pour floods on dry ground, and you are not doing it.' He paused for a while and then concluded: 'God your honour is at stake, and I challenge you to keep your covenant engagements.' At that moment, Duncan Campbell recalls, 'That whole granite house shook like a leaf,' and whilst one elder thought of an earth tremor, Duncan was reminded of Acts 4:31: 'After they prayed, the place where they were meeting was shaken...' Duncan Campbell pronounced the benediction and they went outside. It was about two o'clock in the morning and they found the whole village alive, ablaze with God'. Men and women were carrying chairs and asking if there was room in the church for them!

Brian H. Edwards seeks to bring the reader into contact with revival and to introduce it to those who may never have read much on the subject. This book is not a clinical analysis of revival, nor just an assessment of God's reviving work in the past. Rather, it is the author's declared intention to inform our minds and inflame our hearts so that we may have a heart-longing for God to give us revival in our day and so that we might become what Duncan Campbell describes as a people 'saturated with God'.

The inspiration, authority and history of the Bible **explained**

nothing but the

truth

B R I A N H. E D W A R D S

*Nothing but the truth — The inspiration and
authority of the Bible explained*
Large paperback, 392pp
ISBN 0-85234-305-1
Published by Evangelical Press

The Bible stands alone among books, not only by reason of its long history and great popularity, but because of the enemies it has attracted to itself. From this starting point Brian Edwards sets out to describe the history, authority and accuracy of the Bible in plain, straightforward language designed for the non-expert. Here the author covers such topics as

- Who are the critics of the Bible, and what are they saying?
- What do we mean by inspiration?
- What does the Bible say about itself?
- How sufficient and final is it?
- Why do we have just sixty-six books in the Bible?
- How can we properly understand it?
- When was it written, and how did our English Bible come to us?
- Where does archaeology reveal Bible accuracy?
- What about those supposed errors and contradictions?

A most helpful book.
– *Reformation Today*

Brian Edwards' style is absorbing and simple with technical and theological terms lucidly explained...This book will educate, encourage and inspire its readers.
– *Evangelical Times*

This is an excellent book. Very few books can justly be called invaluable. This book thoroughly deserves the epithet.
– *Banner of Truth Magazine*

Shall we dance — Dance and drama in worship
Small paperback, 154pp
ISBN 0-85234-190-3
Published by Evangelical Press

Over the past decades the use of dance and drama in worship has grown rapidly.

To many, they are an essential part of Spirit-filled worship, for others they present a way to enliven an otherwise dull service, while yet others see them as unwarranted intrusions into the formal worship of a holy God.

So what does the Bible teach about them? Brian H. Edwards looks at these controversial issues and presents a positive message for the church today.

[Brian Edwards'] case is thoroughly researched, well reasoned, and, above all, biblical. Everyone who has responsibility for conducting church worship ought to read this book.
– *Australian Church News*

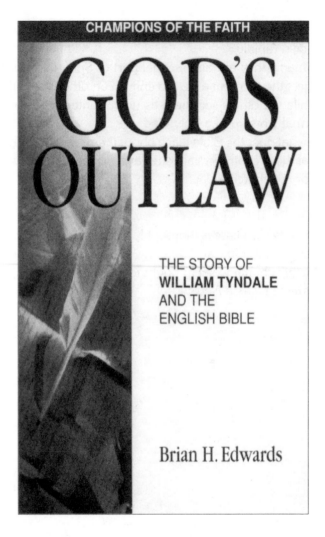

CHAMPIONS OF THE FAITH

GOD'S OUTLAW

THE STORY OF
WILLIAM TYNDALE
AND THE
ENGLISH BIBLE

Brian H. Edwards

*God's outlaw — The story of William Tyndale
and the English Bible*
Large paperback, 192pp
ISBN 0-85234-253-5
Published by Evangelical Press

God's outlaw has every ingredient of a thrilling story — a king, a cardinal, secret agents, a betrayer and a fugitive.

William Tyndale lived in the colourful and cruel days of Henry VIII when men were burned, racked and maimed for lesser crimes than that of smuggling the Bible into England. When Tyndale set out to provide the first printed New Testament in English he was forced to do so in defiance of the king, the pope, and almost every person in authority. Compelled to flee from his homeland, he continued with his work of translating the Scriptures whiles slipping from city to city in Germany, Holland and Belgium in an attempt to avoid the agents who were sent from England to arrest him. His story is one of poverty, danger and ceaseless labour.

This fugitive and outlaw gave the English-speaking people their most priceless heritage: the Scriptures in their mother tongue.

This excellent book has been reprinted numerous times and now comprises part of the *Champions of the Faith* series.

A wide range of excellent books on spiritual subjects is available from Evangelical Press. Please write to us for your free catalogue or contact us by e-mail.

Evangelical Press
Faverdale North Industrial Estate, Darlington, Co. Durham, DL3 0PH, England

Evangelical Press USA
P. O. Box 84, Auburn, MA 01501, USA

e-mail: sales@evangelical-press.org

web: http://www.evangelicalpress.org